Sneedville to Kalamazoo

The Walk That Wasn't

by

John W. Leeger

AuthorHouse™
1663 Liberty Drive, Suite 200
Bloomington, IN 47403
www.authorhouse.com
Phone: 1-800-839-8640

© 2008 John W. Leeger. All rights reserved.

No part of this book may be reproduced, stored in a retrieval system, or transmitted by any means without the written permission of the author.

First published by AuthorHouse 5/19/2008

ISBN: 978-1-4343-8139-2 (sc)

Printed in the United States of America
Bloomington, Indiana

This book is printed on acid-free paper.

All images copyright 2008 by John W. Leeger.

For my Mother

With thanks to Bree, Josh, Lindy, Michael and Paul

And with gratitude to all those I met along the way

—

especially to those who felt compelled

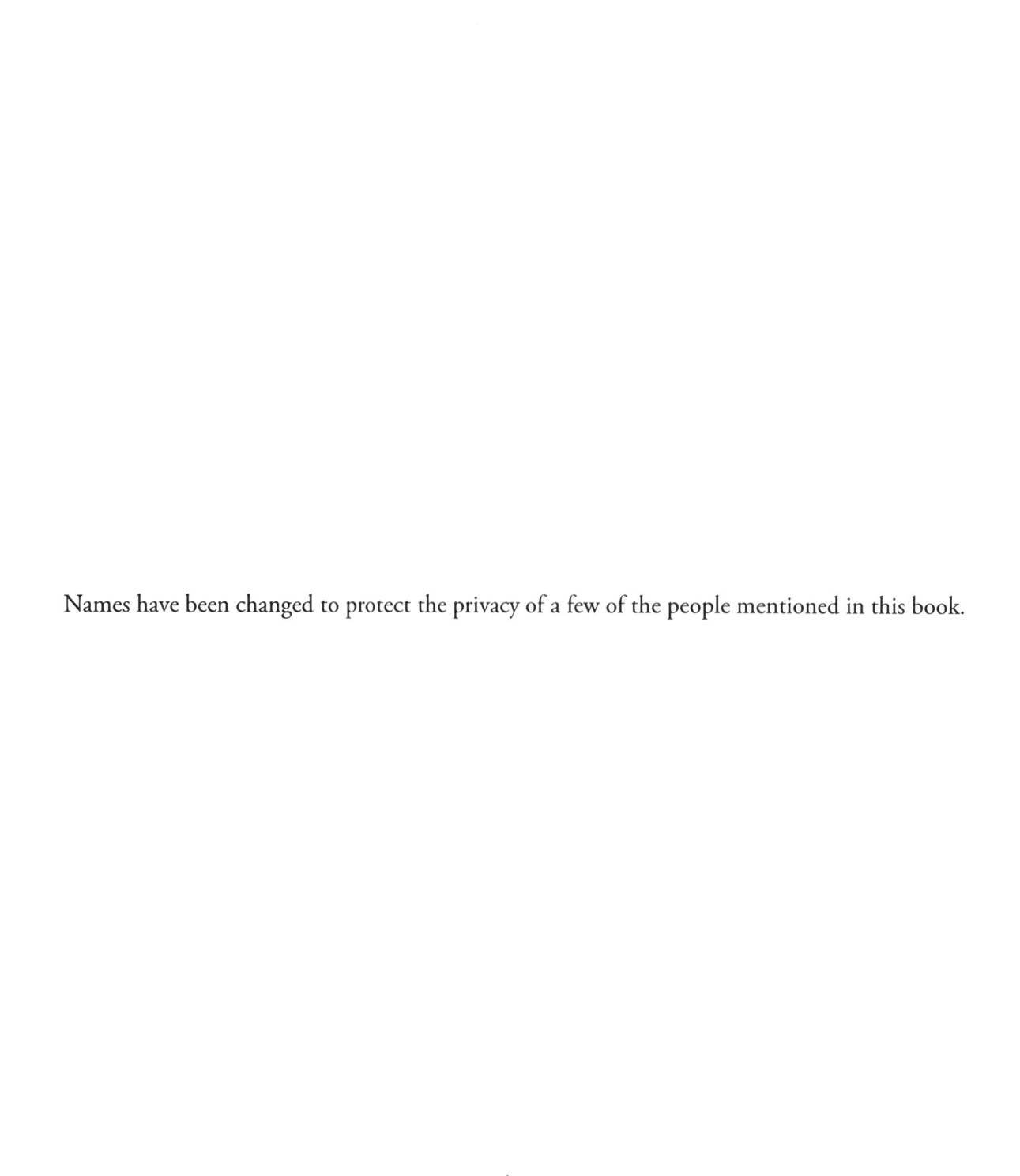

Names have been changed to protect the privacy of a few of the people mentioned in this book.

Prologue

Did you ever want to *really* get away from it all? To leave behind work, family, friends — all the people and things you are *so* familiar with? To put a few essentials in a backpack, and just walk through places you've never walked before, as Heinlein would say, a stranger in a strange land? To get some experience of how and where other people live?

Did you *really*?

Neither did I.

And yet, in the summer of 2007, that's exactly what I found myself doing. I struggled to take a walk I had imagined, and learned, time and again, to let go and accept the ride I was intended to take. I had to learn to let myself be led instead of leading. To see instead of watching. To listen instead of hearing.

I needed to clear the constant babble from my mind in order to hear the still, small voice others have spoken of. Sometimes the voice seemed to be my own, saying things I had heard before but dismissed. On this trip, I tried to listen. Never did the voice tell me to do things that seemed hurtful. Sometimes improbable or unusual. Often not practical or comfortable. But where I followed, I often saw with new eyes. Heard with new ears. Felt with a new heart.

Vision

The vision didn't last very long, but while I was in it, time seemed to stop.

I had driven to Lakewood, outside Cleveland to help my friend celebrate his 60th birthday. "I've got to play the Saturday mass," Wally said, "Why don't you come with me. You don't have to sing — just sit in the loft with us. You can hear the new pastor. He gives a pretty good homily. Then you can leave for home after we get back."

It was Saturday, December 2nd, 2006. I had been there since Thursday and I wanted to be back to sing in my own church, First United Methodist Church of Kalamazoo, the next morning.

It had been an interesting year — in the sense of the ancient curse, "May you live in interesting times."

A year earlier, on Friday, December 16th, 2005, I had returned from The Midwest Clinics, a major trade show in Chicago. By 10:00 that night, I had poured myself a glass of wine and sat down. I put my feet up on the coffee table and thought to myself, "This is great! I'm 61 years old and healthy as a horse. I just spent three nine-hour days standing in my display area talking to hundreds of people. I unloaded my car, carried hundreds of pounds of display, laptop, monitor, samples — all my stuff — in and put it all away. My little business is finally making enough money so that next year it will pay all the bills. Life is good!"

The next morning I awakened sick as a dog. The following Thursday I had surgery to replace the arch of my aorta — 10½ hours with my heart disconnected, my body attached to a multitude of machines, chilled down to a 70° core temperature. In March, the symptoms returned and in mid April I had another open heart surgery — 10 more hours with my heart disconnected again, my body once again attached to a multitude of machines, and once again chilled down to a 70° core temperature — to replace the next section of my aorta down to my diaphragm. The next day, another surgery to remove the tip of the epidural that somehow got lodged in the bottom of my spinal column. In May and June I had withdrawal symptoms that nearly killed me when I stopped taking Hydrocodone (an OxyContin derivative) without asking my doctors how to wean myself from the stuff.

Now, amazingly, I was returning to health. My body still hurt, but increasingly I found myself not being concerned about the pain that signaled it was rebuilding itself. My mind was no longer foggy. Or, some people would say it was back to its original fogginess. At any rate, life was, once again, good.

At least, my physical life was good. Blue Cross / Blue Shield of Michigan had paid about 95% of the $740,000 in medical costs. But what was left on top of the bills I had been juggling was quite a load. Surgeons had warned me that I should never again lift more than 30 pounds. Attending the conventions that produced the bulk of my sales was out of the question. My little company was virtually moribund. I declared personal bankruptcy in the summer.

Still, as a friend of mine said, I was on the right side of the grass....

The church was crowded. It was just a few weeks until Christmas. As it turned out, the new pastor didn't speak that evening. But by the time the nun started the homily, I wasn't paying much attention any more.

Standing in the balcony at the back of the church suddenly, between me and the altar, I clearly saw a bit of my future. Because of all the medical problems, I had missed the annual mission trip I had taken nine times before with my old church in Virginia. I was determined to make my tenth trip in 2007. But now, as if I were transported into a huge video screen, I saw the end of the week I would spend the next year in Sneedville, Tennessee. Around me, dozens of others were getting into their cars to drive back to Centreville, Virginia. And there I was, in a robe and sandals... taking a walk.

There was no voice telling me to "heal the sick" or "preach to the heathen" or any other particular thing. I wasn't told where to go, who to see, or for that matter given any instruction at all. I did, however, feel very strongly the need to walk.

On the way back to his house I told Wally what I had seen and asked, "What the heck was that all about?"

"I don't know," he replied, "You're the guy who's seeing things. You tell me."

I didn't sleep much after that. For the next several weeks I awakened several times a night thinking things like, *"You can't do this!" "You just had not one but two open heart surgeries!" "You're going through personal bankruptcy!" "You don't have any income!" "How will you eat?" "Where will you sleep?"* etc.... etc.... etc.....

Then I awakened several times each night thinking things like, *"Well... why can't you do this?" "You* **might** *die... but then, everybody dies sooner or later." "You won't need any income." "Other people find ways to eat and places to sleep." "You have no other responsibilities." "If not now... when?"*

I remembered that often in my life I would pray something like this. *"I know You're there, Lord. I know whatever You are is incomprehensible to me. I know I'm part of You, Lord... but... wouldn't it be nice if... just once... You... talked to me. Showed me for certain You exist."*

And I finally thought someday I will stand in front of my Creator, and He will say to me, "All your life you told me you wanted a sign. I asked you to do one thing... Why didn't you do it?"

And how could I possibly answer that question?

One day while I was in the middle of all this soul searching I was leaving my daughter's house, Bree asked if I had seen the movie *A Prairie Home Companion*. When I told her I had been meaning to, but hadn't gotten around to it, she handed me a DVD and told me it was due back at Blockbuster the next day. I told her I would watch it that night.

At one point in the movie, Garrison Keillor announces the next act — Miss Jearlyn Steele. The band plays the introduction and Ms. Steele sings:

The day is short.
The night is long.
Why do we work so hard
to get what we don't even want?

I felt like I had been slapped in the face. I closed my mouth. Fumbling with the remote control, I went back and played it again. And again. It was quite a while before I could watch the rest of the movie.

Soon after that, I talked with Josh and Bree, my son and daughter. Both thought I should do it. Neither seemed very concerned that something less than good might happen. Later, I learned that there had been plenty of concern....

Mike Palmer is the Diaconal Minister of Music at First United Methodist Church in Kalamazoo and a good friend. Despite the fact I am old enough to be his father, we are alike in many ways — particularly in our love of choral music. I decided to talk with him first, and then to talk to other people of faith who might provide useful counsel. Before telling any of them about what I had seen, however, I asked each of them what happened to lead them into ministry. Did God come down and smack them upside the head with a big scepter to get their attention? Or did they just sort of drift into the profession.

Several had a definite vision or calling. A couple found themselves on paths that lead them into ministry and then realized they had found their life's work. Eventually, I spoke with six Methodist ministers and a Catholic priest.

Mike had a definite calling. At church one day he clearly saw himself leading worship. It struck him hard and left no room for doubt as to what he would do with his life.

Rev. Dr. Doug Vernon, the senior pastor at Kalamazoo's First United Methodist Church sort of backed into ministry. But once on that path, he soon realized he had found his life's work and never looked back. Doug and I are the same age and have a lot in common. He, too, is a good friend and another whose advice I sought.

Both Doug and Mike suggested that I didn't really need to go walking aimlessly with no discernible purpose. There is plenty of work for someone who wants to help others right in Kalamazoo. I knew that, of course. But the calling wasn't something I could ignore. Sure, it could have been a metaphor. In fact, in the end I decided the robe and sandals thing was more than I could do. Starting down the road in

Tennessee, southwestern Virginia, and West Virginia wearing only a robe and sandals could be a life-ending choice. Whatever faith I had wasn't quite that strong. I decided, perhaps paradoxically, that the attire wasn't important, but the walk was.

When I returned to Ohio in January to see Wally's son Jeff, my godson, sworn in as a firefighter, Wally said, "You need to talk to Father Jim."

"What's a Father Jim?" I asked.

He told me a little about Father Jim O'Donnell. In 2005 he had celebrated 50 years as a priest. I agreed to talk with him, if he could spare the time for me. Wally made an appointment at 6:00 Tuesday evening, January 9th. "I'm going to drive you over there, take you in and introduce you, and then I'm going home. I'm not going to leave my car on the street there. I'll come back and pick you up in an hour."

Father Jim lives in The Flats — definitely not the safest part of Cleveland. The two-story, frame duplex has seen better days, but it's in pretty good shape. Father Jim welcomed me into his little office.

When I asked him how he came to be a priest he said, "When I made my first communion at age seven, I decided to be a priest."

"At age seven?" I asked. "What did you do?"

"I went to the parish priest and told him I wanted to go to seminary," Father Jim continued. "He said, 'Jimmy. I'm going to give you some good advice. Go home and grow up. Live with your family. Go to school. Play sports. Drive cars. Have friends. When you graduate, if you still want to be a priest, come talk to me.' When I graduated, I still wanted to be a priest, so I went to seminary."

Sometime in the 1980s (I guess) he went to his bishop and told him he felt he shouldn't be a parish priest any more. "What do you want to do then, Jim?" the bishop asked him.

"I want to live in the worst parts of Cleveland and minister directly to those whose need is greatest — the homeless, the drug addicts, the prostitutes, the people with no hope...." And that's what he has done ever since.

As he talked, I became aware of the aura that surrounds him. White hair frames his strong, square face. He smiles a lot and speaks softly, but with authority. His hands and body are mostly still. Or maybe they just seem still because I was entranced by the compassion in his eyes. He is a compelling presence.

When I could look around, I saw that some of the wallpaper in the office was peeling off. But on the walls were pictures of Father Jim with Mother Teresa, of Father Jim with Jimmy Carter, of Father Jim doing Habitat for Humanity work. Here is a man who walks the walk.

After I told him why I was there we talked about my faith journey. He asked what I heard when I prayed about it. I told him I didn't hear anything. I never heard anything when I prayed. When he asked me why I thought that was, I told him that I had always had a problem listening.

He asked if I meditated. I told him I had tried, but it would usually end up something like this, *"Ohm mahne padmeh ohm.... Ohm mahne.... ....I've got to write checks today.... ....Then I have an appointment at*

1:00.... And there's that phone call I have to make this afternoon...." It's always been next to impossible for me to find silence in my mind.

He suggested I say Brother Charles de Foucauld's Prayer of Abandonment every day.

> *Father,*
> *I abandon myself into your hands;*
> *do with me what you will.*
> *Whatever you may do, I thank you.*
> *I am ready for all, I accept all.*
> *Let only your will be done in me,*
> *and in all your creatures,*
> *I ask no more than this, O Lord*
>
> *Into your hands I commend my soul;*
> *I offer it to you with all the love of my heart,*
> *for I love you, Lord,*
> *and so need to give myself,*
> *to surrender myself into your hands,*
> *without reserve, and with boundless confidence,*
> *for you are my Father.*

I'm not too much into formulaic repetition, but agreed to read it aloud for him. I found it was very difficult for me to speak by the time I got to the end. The prayer touches me deeply. I have said it every day since. It still resonates with me.

Like Mike Palmer and Doug Vernon, Father Jim suggested that there were many ways I could serve others more effectively than just walking among them.

Wally returned at 7:00 and Father Jim went on to his next appointment that night. He's a remarkable man.

"Hey, Wall," I said in the car, "Father Jim introduced that little black boy as his son, Martin. How does a Catholic priest have a three-year-old son?"

"Well," he replied, "he must have had to ask the bishop for permission to adopt him."

"And the bishop granted his permission?" I asked.

"I don't think Father Jim would have cared much if the bishop gave him permission or not," said Wally.

"Well, what's the deal with Sister Maggie. Does she live there and take care of them or what?" I asked.

"Yep," he said.

Back in Kalamazoo, I called two ministers I knew from Virginia. After serving as pastor at St. Stephens United Methodist Church when I was there, Rev. Sam Nesmith was twice a District Superintendent. And Rev. Tim Tate had been a pastor at Centreville United Methodist Church when I attended there. Each had had strong callings to the ministry. And each gave me advice similar to what I had heard before.

In February, I spoke with Rev. Julie Dix, another pastor at my church. Julie had suggestions on spiritual preparation including Centering Prayer and echoed the sentiments of the other pastors.

Then I talked with Lindy Rose. I had served on the Fine Arts Committee at church with Lindy. She had visited me while I was recuperating from the various surgeries and brought good wishes from her husband and daughter. When I told Lindy about all the pastors suggesting that there were other ways of serving, she said, "But it's the walk, isn't it?" When she said that, she gestured with her open hand, pointing with all her fingers out to one side. My mouth dropped open as I realized that every time I had said I was told to "take a walk," I had made the same gesture. I had, in fact, made that gesture when I told Lindy about the vision. I was stunned. She understood immediately the need for the physical walk itself.

"It is, indeed, the walk!" I exclaimed. Whatever doubt I had about doing this crazy thing left me then and there.

After that, I still didn't sleep much, but I was excited about doing this thing. I assumed that what I had wasn't a gas bubble and that God would show me what to do and where to go on the trip. I decided to just take a couple changes of clothes, my blood pressure medicine, a toothbrush and toothpaste and a couple of other things like that.

Before I left, I would talk with Sandy and Julie, the other two pastors at Kalamazoo. By the time I spoke with them there was no question about whether I was going to go. They were both supportive. Sandy, in particular, was excited about the journey.

I went to see my surgeon Friday, May 4th, and his assistant said the spiral CT scan and sonogram showed no leakage at the replacement aorta parts. There was no sign of infection. My heart valves were all working well, and my heart muscle was pumping strongly. I was just a bit excited!

When I told Dr. Schneider (the Physician's Assistant) about my plans, he said he was really inspired. Then he asked if he could come along. I told him he was about the 15th person who wanted to come long, but the vision was just me.

I bought a bright red Gore-Tex parka. I called it "I am not a deer" red. The idea was to keep me from getting shot if I was still walking during deer hunting season in the fall. When I told Wally I had bought a parka he asked me if I had bought rain-proof pants, too. I told him I would just count on my Levis to stay warm and reasonably dry. He said, "Take it from a mail man. Get waterproof pants to go with the parka."

I couldn't find any that were red, but I bought a pair of Gore-Tex pants that are bright blue. Sure enough, I was to find that the waterproof pants were worth having.

I also had some T-Shirts made up that said:

Take a Walk
Sneedville to Kalamazoo

The shirts were "I am not a deer" red, too. The lettering was white until I asked the T-Shirt company if they had reflective paint. It cost me a little extra, but seemed like a good idea — until I saw the finished product. The reflective stuff in the paint made the lettering look sort of dull, unless there was a bright light shining on them. Then they positively glared white!

I planned to leave Kalamazoo on June 16th. I would visit friends in northern Virginia before the mission team left for Tennessee on the 23rd. Then, on the 30th, when the mission was completed, I would be on the road.

I would try to stay in a hotel around the beginning of each month. I would find a laundry so I wouldn't smell quite so bad (at least for a little while). I would also turn on my cell phone to see if someone had died or some other major emergency had happened. If possible, I'd check my EMail. I'd even send out a status report.

Then I'd turn all that stuff off and hit the road again.

What little plan there was entailed heading north through West Virginia and into Pennsylvania, then turning west and walking along the southern shore of Lake Erie through Ohio and into Michigan. I would stay on the smaller roads, and see what I saw, and learn what I learned.

The best laid plans....

June 30th
Camp Jubilee to Middlesboro, Kentucky

If you head north out of Sneedville, Tennessee, you'll cross over Powell Mountain, then Newman's Ridge. After a lot of twists and turns, and ups and downs, the road will T at the Mulberry Gap Baptist Church. You'll see a stock truck that has been sitting there every time (but once) that I've driven through there during 10 weeks (over 10 years) in Hancock County.

Turn left on Alanthus Hill Road and drive through the beautiful valley that Peggy always says, "…looks just like Ireland." You'll be heading north and west, toward Ewing and Rose Hill in Virginia. Before you get to Virginia though, turn right on the Powell River Road and just a little ways ahead on the left you'll find Camp Jubilee, where Rev. Ron Owens hosts hundreds of Appalachian children every week during the summers. Rev. Ron has graciously allowed the annual Centreville United Methodist Church mission team — as many as 90 of us at once! — to stay there the last week of June for the most recent of the 16 years we've been coming to Sneedville in Hancock County. While we're there, we clean and disinfect the camp buildings so they're ready for campers the day we leave.

Centreville United Methodist Church's annual mission trip to Sneedville, Tennessee began in 1991. I first went along in 1995. I really wanted to return, but in 1996 and 1997 I had one job stop and another begin. I was one of about 50 people who went back in 1998. My friend Dave Williams and I were the *G-Men* — Garbage Men. We drove the truck to the garbage dump every day and did various other smelly jobs that needed to be done.

Tuesday, one of the youth said, "John, you should do Backyard Bible."

We run sort of a Vacation Bible School at several places in and around Sneedville Monday through Friday. She was on the Mountain Team — there was also a Valley Team, and lately a River Team, too — that met in the mornings at the Sneedville Apartments and in the afternoons in the Cope-Collins hollow, way out of town.

"I don't think so," I said, "I do the heavy, dirty jobs — swing the hammer, lift the garbage and stuff. You know — the 'manly' things."

"But you'd be good with the little kids," she protested.

"No..." I said, "I don't think so."

"OK, then..." she said, "I **challenge** you to come to Backyard Bible."

That sounded like the "Double Dog Dare" from the movie, *The Christmas Story*. Not being able to resist something like that, I got Dave to agree and Wednesday we went along with the Mountain Team. I was completely unprepared for how deeply I would feel about the kids. Many didn't have running water at home. Many didn't have at least one parent at home. Many had only one or two sets of clothes, most of which were hand-me-downs.

They were incredibly shy around us at first. Adult men from Centreville hadn't participated in Backyard Bible before. I think the kids were afraid of us. When they finally realized all we wanted to do was sit down and help them put stickers on stuff or color stuff or give them shoulder rides, they were like little leeches. They clung to us, wrestled us to the ground so we could tickle them and they us. They put stickers on us, painted us with magic markers, and just generally treated us like playmates.

When it was time to say goodbye on Friday, all of us — kids and adults — hugged and cried. I know this sounds corny, but if I knew a way that I could adopt 200 or so kids, I would do it in a heartbeat. And so would most of the rest of us.

I went every year after that (until I got sick in 2006) and that week-long trip was one of the most important times of each of those years. Not being able to go in 2006 upset me almost as much as all the operations and hospital time.

I was so happy to be able to return in 2007. When I saw myself in the vision starting the Walk in Sneedville, I felt that trip would help get me together before I set out. I decided not to tell anyone on the mission trip about the vision until the last day when I started walking. I didn't want what I was about to do to detract from the mission.

    Just after we took the annual group picture right before everyone left to drive back to northern Virginia, I told the team members about the vision I had. It was an incredibly emotional time for me and, I think, for the 76 other members of the mission team. Everyone crowded around to hug me and wish me good luck. Someone gave me a couple of apples. I stuck them in my backpack, along with the three power bars my son had insisted I take. There was a lot of bumping and tugging. When I was on the road later, I found people had stuck money in my back pockets. It definitely came in handy, as did the apples.

At about 9:40 I shouldered my backpack and set off up the Powell River Road east toward Jonesville, Virginia. I felt exhilarated. I'm gregarious by nature — OK. I'm a major extrovert. — and couldn't wait to meet new people and to see new things.

The Powell River valley is as lovely as the area around Mulberry Gap. Sometimes after dinner at Camp Jubilee, Dave and I would just sit and look at it. We called it watching MTV — Mountain television.

And when you're on foot, the silence makes it even more entrancing. The hills reached up almost to touch the low gray clouds. I thought I would need my rain parka, but it didn't rain all day. The temperature was warm, but the humidity wasn't too bad. A lovely little breeze helped a lot. It was a wonderful day to be walking!

The last of the mission team members going back to Centreville went by me about 10:00, tooting their horns and waving. After that, I only saw about 12 or 15 cars until 2:40 or so when I crossed into Virginia.

The road didn't have much of a shoulder — only a foot or two and virtually nothing but a ditch in some places. A lot of cars would have made my journey much more dangerous. I tried always to walk facing traffic. From time to time I would find a stretch of road where there was no place to jump on the left side of the road. If conditions were better on the right side, I would walk on there until the left side looked safer. I was always nervous when I couldn't walk facing traffic.

What little route planning I had done involved walking the 19 miles to Jonesville, Virginia, Saturday and going to a little church just west of the town Sunday morning. I thought I had hardened my feet pretty well walking around Kalamazoo for a couple months before leaving for Sneedville, but that, it turned out, was overly optimistic.

When I was a child I twisted my left ankle badly enough so I was out of school for a week or so. In those days there wasn't much that could be done for damaged tendons and muscles. I was prone to spraining that ankle for years. In 2002 an orthopaedic surgeon in northern Virginia did some creative rebuilding there. The ankle has seemed stronger since, but I was unsure of how well it would hold up if I had to jump down into a ditch that might be filled with rocks or garbage or, for that matter, snakes. Accordingly, I had decided to wear boots on the walk. The extra ankle support might prove critical, and any snakes that wanted to nibble on me would have to reach up a little higher to be effective.

In April in Kalamazoo, my old boots gave me some blisters the first time I walked a long way — 12 miles, in fact. So I ordered a new pair. I also ordered a new pair of Happy Feet — gel-filled insoles that I had worn for several years. Until I left in mid-June I walked more and more as the blisters went away.

Of course, I was pretty exhausted from getting up every morning with Dave Williams to wake the rest of the mission team. Staying up until 11:00 or midnight every night to make sure the young people got to bed on time didn't help either, I guess.

An hour or so after leaving Camp Jubilee I found a flat rock on the north side of the road that made a perfect chair. When I sat down for a little break, I discovered that my backpack made a reasonable backrest. It was shady and oh, so peaceful. I didn't quite fall asleep....

Two little churches stand about a quarter mile apart about six miles from Camp Jubilee. By the time I go to Martin's Creek Baptist Church (the first of the two), I was pretty tired. It has a little shelter with some picnic tables. I napped for a couple hours on one of the picnic tables.

Sitting on the table I could see a couple miles to the hills on the north and south sides of the valley. Looking east, I could see the second church about a tenth of a mile down the road.

About 1:40 I walked by the second church, the Wolfenbarger Missionary Baptist Church. There was a pickup truck parked in front of it, but I didn't see anyone, so I didn't stop. After a while I came to a Virginia road sign for Flatwoods Road.

    I hadn't walked very far, but I felt like I had accomplished something by arriving in a second state. There would be more, soon enough….

    Soon I found another chair-sized rock. I was grateful for a place to sit. As I sat down, a two-foot long black snake slithered between my feet under the rock. That gave me quite a start! I was happy it was a black snake living under the rock I chose for a chair and not one of the poisonous varieties. As I looked to see where he had gone, however, I thought my feet were surrounded by poison ivy. Closer examination showed it wasn't poison ivy at all — much to my relief.

This second rock sat in a lovely little valley. When I walked across the road to see what was between the two trees down the precipitous drop past the shoulder, I found a little stream gurgling contentedly. The hillside was choked with vines and bushes and more of the non-poison ivy.

    I thought about the people who had settled here so many years ago, and of the Civil War soldiers who had slogged across little streams like this one. Many of those folks hadn't had shoes of any kind. It wasn't the first or the last time I thought of them.

As I sat there a silver pickup truck drove by heading west. The truck was decorated and had *Just Married* painted on the windows. I waved and gave them two thumbs up. As they went up the hill, they tooted their horn and waved out of both windows. I couldn't get my camera out in time, so I took a picture looking where they were headed, back west down Flatwoods Road, the way I had come. Silently, I wished them a long and happy marriage.

About 5:15, a van from a Baptist church in Greenville, South Carolina stopped across the road from me. Two adults and two youth were going from house to house, spreading the Gospel. They offered me a ride to Jonesville. They were staying at Lincoln University, and had just started their week there. I thanked them and wished them well.

At 20 minutes 'til 6:00 I stopped at the top of the next hill just outside a house that reminded me of the little house where I grew up in Gary, Indiana.

At 6:30 I sat outside someone else's house dozing for a little while. These folks had the yappiest dogs. I didn't think they'd ever stop. They must have been a bunch of hound dogs. Some were baying, some barking.

My feet were hurting. I stopped a couple other times to sit by the side of the road and rest a bit. The feet were a good excuse.

The valley was so beautiful. I found myself staring. I was like a camera with the shutter held open too long — overexposed. There was just too much to see. And of course, there was nothing to see. Nothing extraordinary, at any rate. Just fields and weeds and streams, tree-covered hills and clouds. These words we use to describe things that surround us every day don't begin to express how beautiful they actually are. Maybe Thoreau was on to something....

Just before 7:00 I talked to some folks who were walking their dog by the road. They thought I had another eight miles to go. That was kind of depressing. If I averaged two miles per hour, I wouldn't be in Jonesville until at least 11:00. And I was pretty sure I'd need more rest....

A few minutes later I came to house with a sheriff's car parked out front — across from the great big silo with the silver top. I knocked on the door and asked the guy if I could use his bathroom.

He said, "The bathroom?"

And I said, "Yeah. I'm walking to Jonesville, and I left Ronnie's place...."

"Well..." he interrupted, "...it's a long way to Jonesville."

"OK..." I said, "Never mind." And I left.

I napped for another hour at the White Shoals Missionary Baptist Church until 8:30 or so. There seemed to be a Baptist Church of some sort every couple miles down the Powell River Road.

At 9:15 I ate most of a Power Bar. I had already eaten the apples. The Power Bar was a poor excuse for food. It was so dry I had to wash each bite down with water to be able to swallow it. But my water ran out before I could finish the thing and I was too dry to swallow it without some liquid.

My feet were really sore. I took off my boots and found that the Happy Feet insole in my right boot had burst and scrunched up under my right heel. I had a whopper of a blister there. I put the one from my left boot upside down in the right boot and stuck the bad insole in my backpack.

Limping because of the pain in my right foot was making blisters on my left foot, too. I sat with my feet in the open air for a while. Then I put on clean socks and put my boots back on. That felt a little better, but it still hurt.

Being out of water was not a good thing. I had seen what dehydration can do in previous mission trips. I had brought a filter that would purify stream water, but the last stream was several miles back at the last flat rock I rested on. I hadn't seen a house in quite a while — since before the White Shoals Missionary Baptist Church.

About 9:30 I walked up to a house with all the lights on and knocked on the door. Rhonda and Earl (Campbell, I think) and their two little boys, Honer and C.J., were in the process of moving in. Furniture and boxes were stacked willy-nilly all over the place. As sweaty and dirty as I was, they invited me in and gave me a gallon of water. It was wonderful of them to take time out of their busy day and be so helpful. I plan to stop and talk to them next year on the way back from Sneedville.

By 10:00, my feet were really hurting and I was exhausted. I had come to another house, and decided I wasn't likely to walk much further without some sleep. I had to knock three times on the door before the owner answered. I explained who I was and what I was doing. Then I asked him if I could sleep on his porch or under the big tree in his front yard right next to the road. He looked at me a little funny, but after a pause he said I should sleep under the tree so the dogs wouldn't get me. That didn't make much sense, but I was so tired I didn't care a lot. I laid down under the tree and went right to sleep.

About 10:30 a bright light woke me up. That's when I met Richie Perkins. That is, Sheriff Richie Perkins of the Lee County Sheriff Department. "What do we have here?" he asked, shining his big flashlight in my eyes. He was wearing skin-tight, rubber gloves like the ones used by medical personnel, but black. I guess they were to protect him from whatever might be on me.

I gave him my driver's license and he radioed the information in. While he was waiting for a response, I told him who I was and why I was there. He said he admired me for doing what I was doing. After talking to his office, he told me I wasn't doing anything wrong, but he'd have to drive me into Jonesville.

I think the fellow who owned the house must have thought I was on drugs or alcohol or something and called the police. After all, what would you think if a large, sweaty, dirty guy with a beard and a backpack knocked on your door at 10:00 at night and asked to sleep on your porch? I guess I should be glad he didn't just go get his gun.

I had walked about 15 miles, and now I was riding. This wasn't right, was it? I thought I was supposed to be taking a walk....

Richie told me the county would put me up at a hotel. I was mortified. I hadn't thought about vagrancy laws (although Richie said I didn't qualify as a vagrant anyway). I wasn't allowed in the office, so I sat outside the Sheriff Department while they tried to find a room. There wasn't one in the Jonesville Motor Court, nor was there one in Pennington Gap or Big Stone Gap. That about did it for Lee County.

By now I had met half the sheriffs in Lee County, as well as the dispatcher. She was a life saver. She opened the window between her desk inside and the bench I was sitting on outside, and asked if I was hungry. She offered me a bag full of crackers, apples and baby carrots. Since I hadn't eaten anything but two apples and part of a Power Bar all day, I accepted. She also gave me a half pint of the coldest milk I've ever had. Boy, was it good! The cold carrots went down quickly, too. But the crackers were too dry — even with water from my backpack.

About 2:00 in the morning, Sheriff Sam Flannery told me there weren't any rooms in Lee County, and they were going to escort me out of the county. "Where in West Virginia will that put me?" I asked as I was getting in his car.

"Oh, no," said Sam, "We'll take you to Middlesboro, Kentucky." That, of course, was not the direction I had in mind at all. About 40 miles west, in fact.

About 20 miles west of Jonesville, Sam handed me off to Sheriff Gray Janeway who took me to the Cumberland Tunnel. He turned me over to Officer Roush, an escort at the tunnel. Officer Roush drove me through the tunnel and let me off just west of the tunnel in the Foodway parking lot. That was as far as he was allowed to take me.

He told me where the two closest motels were. He thought the Holiday Inn Express was closer, so I walked there. As he left me in the Foodway parking lot at 2:30 a.m. it started to rain. Hurriedly I got out my parka and my rain pants. It was a struggle getting the pants on, but I couldn't see the Holiday Inn when the rain started, and I didn't want to get soaked.

The mile that Officer Roush claimed it was to the Holiday Inn sure seemed more like two to me. By the time I got there, I was totally exhausted. Through the security window Kim Linton, the night clerk, told me, "I'm sorry, but we don't have any rooms."

I told her a bit of how I had come to be there and said, "Please help me. I don't think I can walk any more tonight. Can you find me a room somewhere?"

She came around and opened the lobby door. She told me to sit down and showed me where the bathroom was. She offered me coffee and said she would see what she could do.

When I came out of the bathroom, she told me she hadn't been able to get the other motels to answer their phones. I offered to pay her to let me sleep in the lobby if she could get me a room for Sunday night, too. Thank goodness, Kim was able to shuffle the three rooms held for early arrivals and put me in one for two nights. So at 4:00 in the morning I found myself staying in a Holiday Inn.

Not at all what I had pictured. I had naively thought people or churches would provide places for me to sleep and eat. Or that I would find shelter where homeless people slept. Sheriff Perkins had explained to me that things didn't work like that in Lee County, Virginia. And Officer Roush informed me they didn't work that way in Middlesboro, Kentucky either. My feet hurt so much I wasn't inclined to wander around until I found a safe-looking place to curl up.

I examined my feet, and wasn't very happy with what I saw. Maybe a good night's sleep would help. I took a shower, hung up my wet clothes and, after setting the alarm clock, went to sleep.

July 1st
Middlesboro, Kentucky

When I checked in, I asked Kim where the nearest church was that might have a van to pick up visitors. She directed me to the Baptist Church behind the WalMart. After taking a shower and sleeping for a couple hours, I called the church, but no one answered. My feet were in no condition to walk a mile or two, so I looked in the phone book and found Covenant United Methodist Church — the only Methodist Church in town. Not only did they answer their phone, but Brenda Stoneburner came right over to the motel and picked me up.

My intention that Sunday had been to go to the little Baptist Church in Jonesville, Virginia I had driven by so many times going to and coming from Sneedville. The condition of my feet precluded walking too far, so I opted for a Methodist church. That's the denomination of my home church. After that first service, I decided to look for Methodist churches wherever I was on following Sundays, just to see what differences there were.

Covenant United Methodist Church is a lovely building. The sanctuary is circular (OK, it's octagonal.) and is an appealing mix of wood and stone. I liked the way the trusses and gables seemed to reach for the heavens.

Rev. Dr. Philip D. Hill preached, and on 4th of July weekend, he came out strong for putting God — make no mistake, the God of Christians — back in the forefront in the United States. The title of his sermon was *Can You Take God from America Without Forming Another Nation?* I found the selection of hymns interesting. It had been a long time since I had sung *"Marching to Zion"* in a worship service, let alone, *"America,"* and *"America the Beautiful."* The postlude was *"God of Our Fathers."*

The bulletin informed me that one of their families had moved to Tazewell, Tennessee — near Sneedville. Tazewell is only about 15 miles from Middlesboro, but that might be a tough commute in winter.

After the service, Brenda and her husband Wendell offered to drive me back to the motel. On the way, Wendell asked if I would like to go to lunch with them, since they normally go out to lunch after church.

We went to Randy's, next door to the motel. The food was just OK, but the company was good. Wendell is an Elder in Residence at Covenant and Brenda is the Director of Children. They commiserated about my feet and encouraged me in my endeavor. It was a good time.

No sightseeing for me. I spent the rest of the day with my feet elevated, drifting in and out of sleep and trying to find something to keep my mind occupied.

July 2nd – July 4th
More Middlesboro, Kentucky

I left the Holiday Inn at 8:40 on Monday morning. But I guess Saturday had pretty much wrecked me, because I didn't get 15 minutes away and I was tired enough to have to stop and sit down. I made about three miles — stopping a lot. Those three miles took me three and a half hours!

I was pretty delirious sitting outside the Pilot truck stop. I had gone in to use their bathroom. While I was inside, I bought a bottle of Power Ade and a roll. It was already hot outside, but there was no place to sit in the air-conditioned comfort, so I found a shady spot on the sidewalk just in front of the place.

I sat on the sidewalk outside with my Power Ade and cheese Danish, and started spacing out. Things were not looking the way they should. My vision was kind of goofy, and I didn't feel good at all. After about an hour or two of just sitting there, an employee named Curt came outside. We talked for a couple of minutes. He was born in Detroit, but has lived all over the place. Now he's a maintenance guy at the Pilot truck stop. He said, "I've gotta take someone up the road. There's really nothing between here and Pineville up here about 10 miles. If you want, I'll give you a ride up there."

I said, "Ohhhh…." So, I said, "Well, if you can…."

He said, "Well, it'll be about an hour here. You just sit here and I'll come back in about an hour."

I sat there spacing out….

                    spacing out……..

                                  spacing out…………

Finally, after about two hours in la-la land, I came to my senses and said to myself, "Well, wait a minute. There's no Curt here."

The girl at the counter inside said he had gone to the doctor or something. He must have forgotten me, or had second thoughts about giving a large, sweaty, hallucinating man a ride.

I went back outside and sat on the sidewalk for a while longer. I realized there was not going to be any more walking for me today, and from what they said, there was nothing past there for quite a long way.

I was beginning to feel a little like I did after the surgeries the year before when I had stopped taking Hydrocodone and had all the drug imbalances. That worried me. I thought there ought to be some way I could rest and get myself back in shape before I went on. So I went back inside and asked if they could call the state police and have them take me back to the Holiday Inn or something. They wouldn't do that, but she called Marsee's Taxi — the one taxicab in town. For five dollars they drove me back to the Holiday Inn and I checked in there again. I stayed there through Wednesday, July 4th, doing absolutely nothing.

Wednesday, the 4th, I walked over to the WalMart to have a prescription refilled and went to a coin operated laundry to wash my clothes, but other than that and one meal out both days, I stayed off my still-aching feet and slept a lot on Tuesday and Wednesday.

It seemed every time somebody said someplace was a certain distance, the actual distance was always just about twice that. The lady downstairs said the coin operated laundry was about a mile away. I would bet it was at least two — maybe a little more.

I met Billy Otis over at the Coin Op Laundry, and we talked about the state of America. He has driven trucks all over the country — in about a dozen cities spanning both coasts, north and south and everyplace else. He said, "You know I used to believe in the things the Republican Party stands for, but I hope those bums don't get reelected for another 20 years." I was surprised to hear something like that from someone who otherwise looked and acted like a staunch conservative.

I don't normally watch television, so I spent a lot of time in solitude. I started feeling like I felt in the hospital after all the surgeries in 2006 — listless and unfocused. Every once in a while I would turn on the idiot box. Every time I did, however, I ended up turning the thing off in disgust. Even the History Channel's and National Geographic's offerings were so loaded with commercials that I couldn't watch for long. Whether I wanted to or not, I ended up spending a lot of time thinking about all manner of stuff. OK... meditating, if you will.

After the two heart operations I found myself thinking a lot about how tenuous our hold is on life. And the drug imbalances forced me to admit our grasp of reality is easily loosened, too. I had rarely thought of what my place might be in the great scheme of things. Now, those questions were haunting me again. And on top of them, I was having doubts about this trip. Although the vision didn't say anything about where I should stay, I inferred I should be staying in shelters or with people who offered me rooms. Well... there were no shelters, and the only people offering me rooms were sheriffs. So, was I doing the wrong things? Could I have done anything differently? As much as I thought about it, I couldn't think of what else I could have done. Eventually, I stopped thinking about it.

In a more practical vein, I decided I had packed a lot more than I should have and needed to lighten my load. I figured I wouldn't need the three long-sleeve T-Shirts I had brought along until September or October, and I had too many sets of underwear and regular T-Shirts as well. So I put together a box. Judy Hall, the motel manager, sent that and some other stuff to my mother.

Independence Day was anticlimactic for me. I was still groggy on Wednesday, July 4th. One time I woke up, I could hear fireworks somewhere nearby, but looking out the hotel window, all I saw was clouds. I just went back to bed.

July 5th
Middlesboro to London, Kentucky

I left Middlesboro (again) Thursday morning at 7:20 and made it to the same Pilot truck stop by 8:20 — one hour to walk what had taken me three and a half hours on Monday. I rested for about 15 minutes and headed out, determined to make Barbourville, the next town down the road.

Route 25 is still a four-lane, divided highway there. It isn't a limited-access road, but traffic had been pretty heavy. The traffic thinned out a bit as I made my way up the hill past the truck stop. The morning sun was warm, giving promise of considerably more heat later in the day. The humidity was up, too. Other people may perspire a bit, but on hot days, I sweat. And I was definitely sweating already.

About an hour out of the Pilot truck stop a fellow named Freddy Saylor pulled up next to me in his little white pickup truck. Freddy had seen me walking when he was driving east. When he came back west, he stopped and insisted I ride with him a ways. The blisters were acting up again, so I took him up on his offer.

He wanted to know why I was walking by myself. I told him about the vision I had and about all the medical problems I had in 2006.

Freddy said that he couldn't see out of his left eye and he'd had an operation to have part of his intestine removed. He pulled up his T-shirt to show me his scar. I didn't show him all the scars I had accumulated the year before.

He talked about how his faith had sustained him through the rough patches in his life. I enjoyed talking with him. He drove to the BP truck stop just outside of Barbourville and let me out there. I stayed long enough to use the bathroom, and set off again.

At about 10:50 it started to rain. Fortunately, it started so gradually I was able to get my rain gear on before it rained in earnest. At about 11:50 I stopped at a gas station/restaurant and had a cheeseburger. The rain had stopped by then, but it was good to sit for a while and dry out. The Gore-Tex parka and pants kept the rain off me, but in the heat I sweated a lot. I wondered if I might have been drier to just get rained on. I left the rain gear on nevertheless.

As I was leaving, I looked over the counter and saw a dog walking around in the kitchen of the little restaurant at the gas station, sniffing the bags of hamburger buns and other provisions on the lower shelves. None of the workers seemed concerned. The dog probably belonged to the owner of the place. Definitely not like home….

The sky remained overcast — clouds scraping the ridges that fenced in the highway. This wasn't like the flat-bottomed Powell River valley in Tennessee. The road was seldom level. I was almost always walking uphill or down. I'm sure the cars and trucks hardly noticed the long but not-too-steep risings and fallings, but I was certainly aware of them. It gave me pause to remember how much steeper were the hills I would have been walking in West Virginia, if it hadn't been for Sheriff Richie Perkins over in Lee County, Virginia.

At about 1:50 it started to drizzle again. I was next to a place called MO-CAR, LLC. In addition to used cars, MO-CAR sells pre-fab aluminum shelters. I asked a fellow showing a customer a car if I could sleep for a half hour or so under the demo shelter they had in the yard — just until the rain played itself out. He said, "You go right ahead."

When I woke up, about 2:30, I went in the MO-CAR office and introduced myself properly to Carson "Cooch" North who had told me I could nap under his shelter. I should mention that Carson is an honorary Kentucky Colonel. The certificate is up on the wall over his desk.

Carson didn't seem at all surprised when I told him what I was doing and why. He seemed to think it wasn't unusual for someone to decide to walk hundreds of miles because of something only he had seen. I thanked him for letting me rest there and then turned to leave.

As I was leaving MO-CAR, a fellow walked in. I said hello as I held the door for him. A mile or so up the road a little red car pulled over next to me. The fellow I had seen going into Carson's office asked, "Did the Lord say you had to walk all the way to Kalamazoo? Do you have to walk every step?"

I said, "Uh… well… I don't know." As good as it sounded, it seemed to me that I would be abandoning my vision. Already I had been made to take a ride by the Sheriffs in Lee County, and just this day Freddy Saylor had given me another ride. What was happening to the "walk" I thought I was supposed to take?

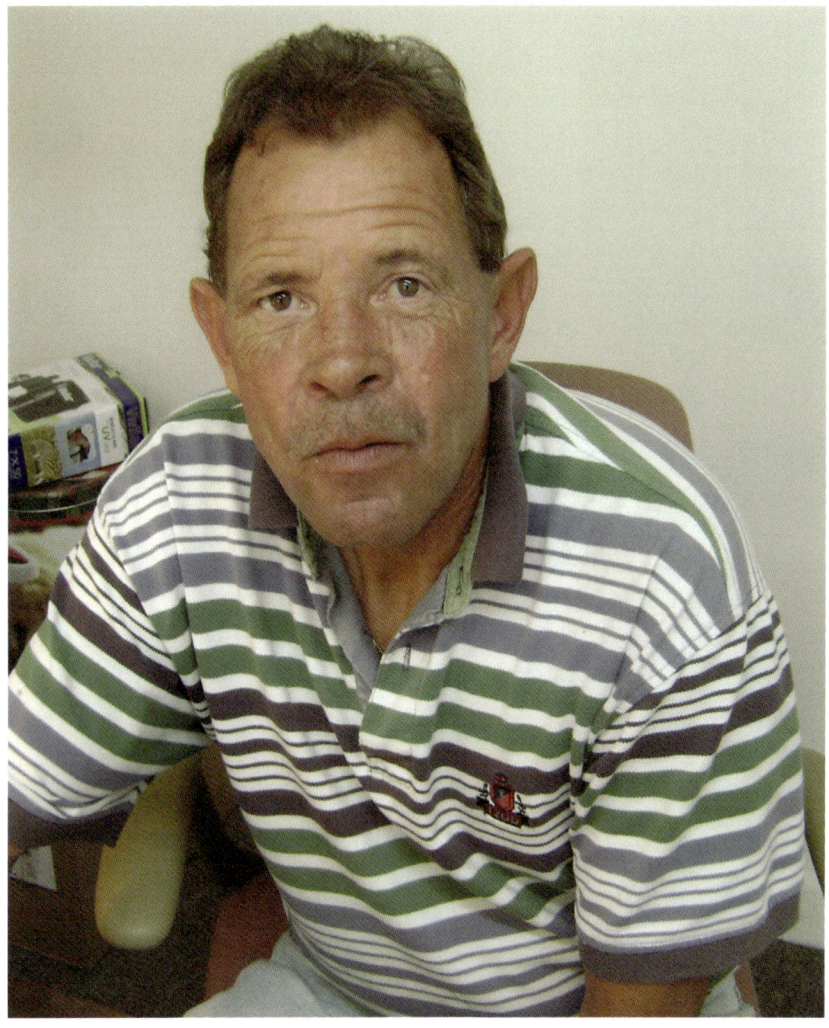

"Cooch told me a little about what you're doing," he said, "I'd kind of like to hear your story. Why don't you get in the car and I'll give you a ride for a while."

"Uh…" I answered, "where are you going?"

"Well," he said, "I'm going up near to Corbin."

"Well… OK," I replied.

The man's name is Bill Hammons. He owns the MO-CAR, LLC place. He worked most of his life up near Flint, Michigan for Chrysler. He grew up in Kentucky near Barbourville — actually, closer to Corbin.

He has had two multiple bypass heart surgeries. He is an alcoholic who's in AA. He piddled along at about 40 miles an hour or so, and we talked and talked and talked. He told me about an experience he had. After his first heart surgery, they had to open him up again to fix a place that was leaking. While he was under the anesthesia, he saw his mother and other relatives behind her, and saw a forearm and hand that reached out and touched him. His mother said, "What are you doing here, Billy? It's too early for you to come. You have to go back."

He said he looked down and, "...I saw myself split open from…" well, he pointed to his chest, right down his sternum — the way I was split open. Then he said, "And I never would have dreamt anything like that." Later, when he got well, he saw pictures of the same sort of operation that he had, with the same chest opening thing that he and I had. He said it looked just like what he had seen while he was "dead." Since then, he sometimes feels a burning in his chest – John Wesley would have said a warming of the heart — when he feels the Lord touches him.

He talked more than I talked, which my friends will tell you is kind of hard to believe.

When we got to Corbin he couldn't find the business he was looking for. "I'm going to have to go up the road here up to London," he said, "Do you want to go to London? I've got to get a part for my swimming pool pump."

"Well… uh, I guess," I answered.

Bill drove me to the Holiday Inn Express next to Interstate 75. He said, "Now, you can't take Route 25 like you were telling me you were going to because it goes out of town a few miles and ends. So you need to get past that to someplace north of that."

When we drove up to the Holiday Inn I said, "I'd like to take your picture, and make sure I have your name spelled right. Is that OK?"

Then, standing outside his car, he said, "Let me pay for your first night and dinner here at the hotel."

"No, thanks," I said, "That's alright. I've got money."

"No," he said, "No. I insist," and handed me a one hundred dollar bill. When I tried not to take it he said, "No. No. Please take this. I'm inspired by your story. I think both of us had something to say to each other and I want to do this for you."

"Well… OK, then…" I said, "you did."

So I ended up in London, Kentucky. He drove me probably 40 miles or so, and at least 10 miles out of his way, going up Route 25 looking for the place that had the part he needed for his swimming pool. It wasn't on that road, so after he dropped me off, he had to go back to Corbin to find it.

From what he said about Route 25 petering out north of London, I was determined to get a better map to see which direction to go from London. I had been using a little tourist map I got at the Holiday Inn Express in Middlesboro for reference. It wasn't very accurate, I had found.

I decided to stay there through Sunday night. Even though one of the blisters on my right heel was killing me, I had walked at least 10 miles that day….

But, hey! I was in London and I was alive and life was good! And once again this journey had turned in a direction that I never would have imagined. Whatever the trip was becoming, I felt fortunate to have met Bill Hammons. He's an inspirational guy. Well, anyway… my notes got a little teary here.

As I was checking in I talked for a few minutes with Jack and Marie Harper[1]. They were returning to Midland, Michigan from a wedding in South Carolina. In my room, later, sitting in a chair with my shoeless feet propped up on the bed, I thought about how soon they would be back in Michigan, and when I might get back home.

It seemed like it might be a long, long time….

July 6th – 8th
London, Kentucky

I spent Friday and Saturday staying off my feet. I felt like I was wasting two more days. Of course, there was no schedule — not even a route, as I had learned the first day. Still I was unhappy with more idleness. The idiot box continued to stare balefully at me. I turned it on once in a while, but it was never on for long....

I found the First United Methodist Church of London, KY in the phone book. The town map at the hotel desk showed the church about a mile away. It's actually almost 1.5 miles, but who's counting?

It was a beautiful day for a walk. I left in plenty of time to get to the church early. It's a beautiful old brick building right in the heart of town.

I was early for the service, but the front door was open. It was very quiet. I could just hear voices coming from a doorway on the far side of the sanctuary. Probably the Sunday School, I thought. In the little vestibule I signed the guest book. When I turned the corner into the sanctuary I was confronted by a banner that stopped me cold.

THE SIGN OF GOD IS
WE ARE LED
WHERE WE
DID NOT
PLAN TO GO
HYMNAL
HOLY BIBLE

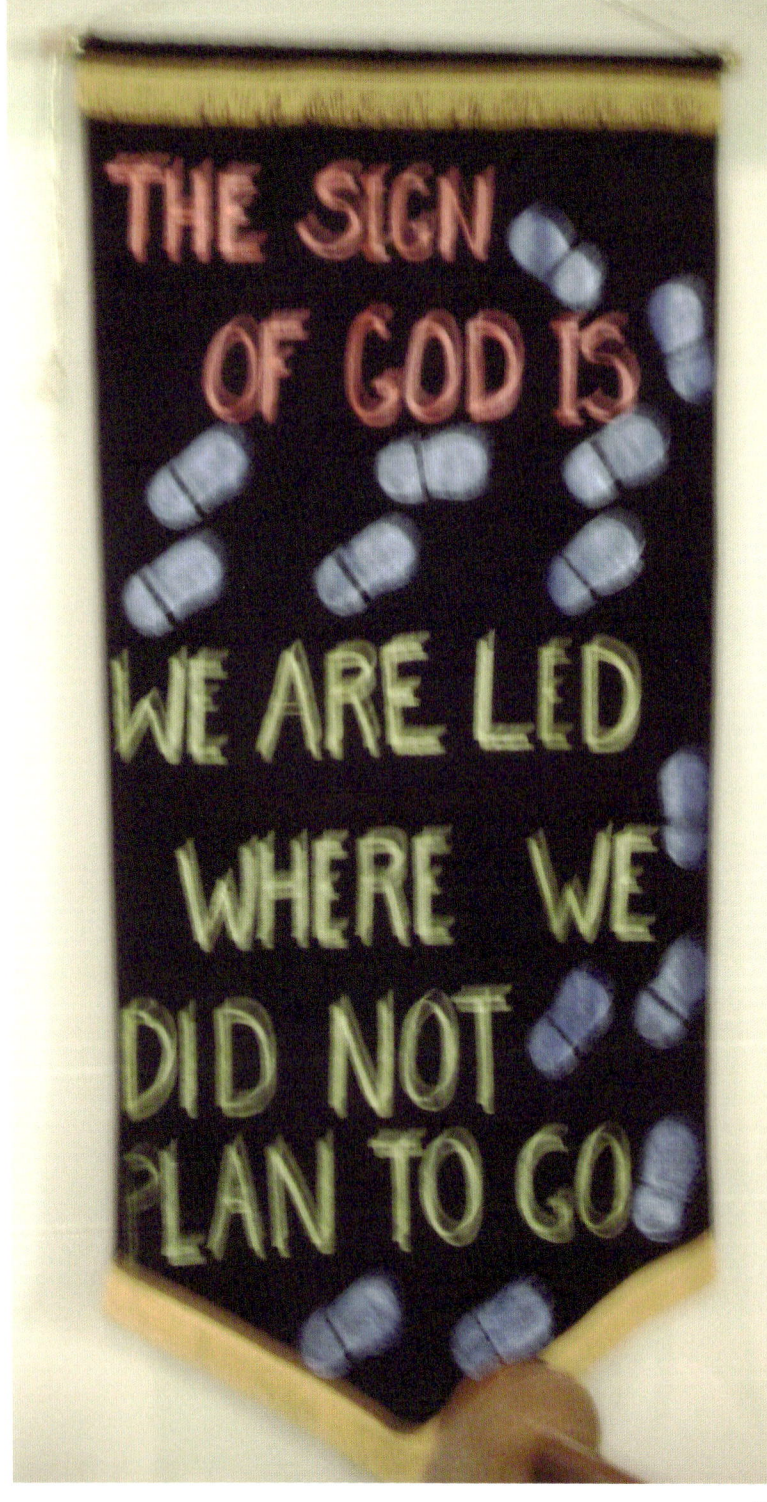

THE SIGN OF GOD IS WE ARE LED WHERE WE DID NOT PLAN TO GO

After all the changes to what I had imagined my trip would be, the message really hit home with me. I took a picture of the banner, but I was sure I was shaking a bit. So I took another. When I was finally able to see the pictures clearly, I found I had been shaking when I took them both.

I must have looked like a fish out of water. I stood staring at that banner for a long, long time.

Coincidence? Some would say so. I tried to convince myself that's all it was. I had been belaboring myself about taking rides. "Take a Walk" is what I heard... wasn't it?

No... I had to admit I hadn't heard a voice saying to take a walk. I had just felt a need to take a walk. Nothing and no one had told me to **walk** back to Michigan. For that matter, even the "back to Michigan" part had been my decision. So what **was** going on here?

Was this whole thing my own concoction? I had to admit, much of what I was doing was based on decisions I had made. One of the first things I had changed from the vision was not to wear a robe and sandals. That, I had convinced myself, was not meant to be taken literally — it was just a symbol. But then, couldn't the whole thing have been just a symbol?

Maybe. But the vision itself **was** real. It **had** happened. What it meant, I still wasn't clear on, but I knew that something had happened. Something that demanded that I do... something.

The nights I spent in hotel rooms had been filled with this sort of tail-chasing logic. About all I had concluded was that I would keep plugging along until it all made sense.

Somehow.

And now... now this....

This provided another solid kick in the pants. I would keep on going, but would be more open. I would pay attention to intuition. I would listen... and look....

When I had regained my composure, I walked around the church, starting with the sanctuary. There is a beautiful Storey and Clark pump organ as well as a piano. The music was good, but I was disappointed that they didn't play the organ in the service that day.

Light pouring through the stained glass windows burnished the fine woodwork in the sanctuary, imbuing the room with a warm glow that pictures just can't capture. The pews are gracefully curved and must have been built especially for that room. On first glance, the pulpit appeared to have been carved from a single piece of oak, but on closer examination I could see some of the craftsmanship that created that illusion.

Rev. Dr. Terry Faris[2], the District Superintendent, spoke on that day. The normal pastor, Rev. Wade Arp, was on a mission trip to Jamaica with 15 parishioners. I was impressed by that. Only about 35 people attended the service on July 8th. If their normal attendance is about 50 people, nearly one third of the parishioners had gone on this mission. Of course, if you're cynical you might attribute that to the fact that the destination was Jamaica. On the other hand, Jamaica is probably more inviting when it isn't July....

Dr. Faris is a wonderful speaker. He stressed that Christianity can be summed up with the acronym *FLOWS* — *F*aith, *L*earning, *O*utreach, *W*orship, *S*ervice. A very emotional man, Dr. Faris had just returned from Africa — Burundi, I believe. He pointed out that if God is my father and God is your father, that makes us brothers. All of us. Around the world.

He made sure we understood that 120 children would die of malaria during the one hour worship service this morning, and stressed how many could be saved with mosquito nets.

A wonderful man, and one who is constantly in service to his fellow man. One more reason to be thankful.

After the service we spoke for a while in the parking lot, and I took his picture. Don't let the avuncular look fool you. His grip is strong — like a carpenter, or a wrestler. Doesn't he look like someone who would wrestle with an angel? Or, with a devil, if need be....

He gave me the cross he was wearing. One of his parishioners makes them for him. I wore it throughout the rest of the trip.

July 9th – 10th
London to
Mt. Vernon, Kentucky

Monday morning, July 9th, at about 6:20 a.m., Sam Nesmith called me. He had just returned from a mission trip to Russia, saw my EMails and called, hoping my phone was on so we could chat. It was good to hear from him — a great way to start the week.

Just after 9:00 I turned off my cell phone, left the Holiday Inn in London, and walked through town — about three miles or more. I sat down in a Burger King at the edge of town for a half hour or so, then headed out.

Just outside of town Route 25 had narrowed to two lanes and the traffic wasn't as heavy. On the other hand, shoulders on the road were minimal. Now and again I would encounter sections where the guard rails on both sides of the road were just a foot or so from the pavement. When that happened, I would stop by the end of the guardrail on the left side of the road and watch the traffic in both directions until it looked like I could make it to the other end of the guard rail without making traffic stop. I walked much quicker through those stretches....

Going up the hill (It felt like a mountain to me!) north of town, I stopped at the driveway of the Family Counseling Center to rest. Looking across the way I saw railroad tracks and a little field with cars going by now and again. I napped for a little while and then started walking again. My right heel still hurt. But the temperature cooled down a little bit and there was a lovely little breeze.

A little after 2:00 I took my boots off, took my socks off, turned my socks inside out, put some talcum powder inside them, put them all back on, and laced everything up. I sprayed some bug spray on and set off again. It still wasn't too hot out. It was kind of humid, but there was still a little breeze.

County trucks went by painting the center stripe on Route 25. The traffic slowed down to a crawl. There still hadn't been any restaurants or any place to get something to eat and I was getting hungry.

Just past a volunteer fire station at the top of the hill is a building with a shady porch. It's next to a medical center where State Route 490 merges into Route 25. The building was empty, so I figured no one would care if I rested in the shade for a while. I sat there and dozed for a few minutes before hitting the road again.

After a while I came to Snuffer Cemetery. What a name! I sat under a tree next to the entrance driveway and rested for a half hour until 3:30. Then I set out again.

By the time it was 4:00, I was pretty pooped again — hot and sweaty. I stopped under a tree for a while to get out of the sun and then walked again. It seemed like the intervals between rest stops were getting shorter and shorter.

By 4:20, I probably had a little more than a quart of water left in my backpack, and I didn't seem to be getting to a place where I could sleep or eat or anything. I didn't know what to do next, so I decided just to walk to the next place — whatever that might be.

At 10 minutes 'til 5:00 I sat for a while on a little stone bench in front of the Calvary Baptist Temple in East Burnstadt, Kentucky. The pastor's kids playing over by the side of the church said they didn't think there was a restaurant for a long time heading west. They said their mother was home next door. I hesitated for a while, but eventually went over and knocked on the door.

Through the screen door, another of Pastor Perry's boys said he thought it was about 15 miles to Livingston, the next place there might be a restaurant. I didn't know what to do except keep walking, but everything was hurting.

By 6:00 I had pretty much given up hope of getting any place that night. I was exhausted. I knew I was near the entrance to the Daniel Boone National Forest, with about 15 more miles to get to the other side. I was sure there wouldn't be any place to eat there. I could sleep on the ground — assuming the local sheriffs wouldn't object — but my feet wouldn't be too much better the next day. I wasn't sure I could make 15 miles without finding at least a place to eat.

It was an hour back to the Calvary Baptist Temple, and there hadn't been any other place since then where I might ask for something to eat. I didn't know what to do. My "walk" had already been compromised and there wasn't about to be much more walking this day....

I looked west to where the National Forest awaited. It seemed dark and foreboding that direction. I felt weary — whatever reservoir of strength I had been drawing on was nearly empty.

I looked back the way I had come. The thought of retracing my steps was disheartening.

"OK, God," I said, "I don't know what to do here." Looking up, I said, "I guess I'm going to stick my thumb out and see if somebody will drive me through the forest. I'll stand here until 6:30. If nothing happens by then, You and I will need to talk."

There wasn't much traffic in either direction. The drivers of the few cars that passed didn't seem to notice me at all. After all that braggadocio, what would I say to God? And then, what would I do?

And then, at the stroke of 6:30, Matthew Warren pulled over and picked me up. He had left London at 7:00 in the morning to drive to work near Mt. Vernon, about 30 miles northwest of London. Now, after a long day at work, he had been heading southeast to go home.

He said he never picked up hitchhikers, but when he drove by me he "felt compelled" to turn around and come back and offer me a ride. I stared at him, mouth agape. He didn't seem to notice. I'm sure the silence only lasted a second or two, but to me, it seemed much longer.

He asked where I was going. When I told him I was trying to get to a restaurant and a place to sleep, he offered to drive me where he had been heading — to London. I thanked him, but said I just couldn't go back there and then have to walk the 14 miles back the next day. And then, not only did he offer me a ride, but he drove me all the way to Mt. Vernon — the opposite direction from where he was headed. That was rather stunning.

Matthew drove me through the Daniel Boone National Forest. That was really a Godsend. As I rode, I took notice that there was nothing between the eastern edge of the forest where he picked me up and the west. Occasionally there would be a house, but they looked like they didn't have anyone living in them. As I expected, there just wasn't much civilization there at all.

Matthew dropped me off at a KFC restaurant just before 7:00. After I had something to eat, I walked down the hill to the Days Inn at the Renfro Valley exit off Interstate 75 on U.S. 25 heading north. Perhaps "walked" is a bit optimistic. My feet were killing me.

I decided to stay in the Days Inn for a day. The blister on my right foot had pretty much covered almost the entire heel which was not encouraging. I cut off a big chunk of blister from the ring toe (ring finger?/ring toe?) of my right foot. It was about the size of a dime and came from my little, teeny, tiny toe, so I guess it had covered that whole toe. That part felt better, but the heel was still pretty miserable. The blister on my right heel was about the size of a dollar bill folded in half. It wrapped around the right side of my heel. A ridge of skin stuck off the back of my heel like the heel of a shoe. It was pretty disgusting to look at.

To add insult to injury, limping to minimize pain on my right heel had created a set of blisters at the front of my left foot. By now, they were every bit as painful as the blister on my right heel. None of this was good news....

The next morning, I had a little breakfast at the hotel office. Then, I was prepared to be bored all day because there was absolutely nothing to do in the hotel room except rest my foot. And there was no question that my foot needed resting. I decided not to turn the phone on, and there was no Internet access there. That was probably just as well.

At about 2:00 I hobbled across the parking lot to Denny's to have dinner or lunch or supper or whatever — all of that stuff wrapped up together. Brittney Schalk, my waitress (to my left in the picture), asked me about my T-Shirt. She, in turn, told the other staff members what I was doing. Most of them were taking a lunch break since it was between shifts. Before I left they all came over, three or four at a time. I had to tell the story over and over again. That was fine with me.

Jessica Stallsworth, the manager, paid for my lunch, which was awfully nice. Someone who had just come in took a picture of the whole staff with me in the middle of them. I was humbled. These are very nice, very pleasant people. They were all excited about what I was doing. It was an emotional time.

I went back to the motel and cut off even more of the blister on my, uh, let's call it the fourth toe on my right foot. So it was a little sensitive still. And my heel was still a mess. I tried to take some pictures of it, but I won't share those here.

I woke up in the middle of the night (again) and realized I hadn't included this story from the Sneedville mission. I believe it was Friday, June 29th, before dinner at Camp Jubilee that for some reason, I felt compelled to talk to Matt Osborn about my trip before I talked to everyone else. Matt is a student at West Virginia Wesleyan College, studying to be a Methodist minister. I got to know Matt when he had helped Dave and me with the wake up calls at Camp Jubilee. That night, we sat in Kallapos's van and talked for half an hour, I guess. I told him about the vision and what I intended to do. We talked about all sorts of things, and then he said, "I want to give you something. Let me run down the hill. I've got something I want to give you."

I tried to tell him that wasn't necessary, but he said, "No. No. I want to give you something." I said, "OK."

And so he ran down the hill and when he came back he gave me a little silver fish — one of the earliest symbols of Christianity — with five Greek letters on it (ΙΧΘΥΣ) that symbolize faith in Christ.[3]

Matt said, "Now... this is just a loan. I want it back. And I don't want it sent to me in the mail. I want you to give it to me in Sneedville next year." And he said, "I want you to pray with it every day."

And so I have. But I had been worried about losing it, because it's just a skinny little thing. I had kept it in the watch pocket of my jeans, but it occurred to me when I awoke that a better place for it would be on the lanyard that holds the cross that Terry Faris gave me. So that's where I put it, and I will keep it there until I see Matt next year.

While I was in the Holiday Inn in London I had an EMail from a friend I haven't seen in years. In it he said, "Something has been telling me to send you this. Hope it helps. Write when you can." The note accompanied his payment of $100 to a PayPal account in my name. I didn't even have a PayPal account, but I thanked him very much. I replied, "Thanks, Dave. I have money, but I appreciate you doing this. I'll just leave it there, and maybe someday I'll need it."

It occurred to me that the room charge at the Days Inn in Mt. Vernon was $45.10 a night — the lowest rate the desk clerk could give me. And I would have bet a nickel that by the time the tax was added on in the morning when I checked out, that $100 will have pretty much exactly covered the two nights at the Days Inn.

July 11th
Mt. Vernon to Berea, Kentucky

Thursday I got up early, took a shower and soaked my feet. When they were real dry, I did a major Mole Skin patch around my right heel. This was an exercise in futility. You're supposed to put Mole Skin around a blister to keep pressure off the blister. This blister was so large, however, that there wasn't much space that was blister-free. I did my best.

And then, after I hobbled over to the motel office and had breakfast, I hobbled out of town. Hobbling, it seemed, was going to be the basic mode of transportation for a while. It rained like the dickens the day before, and promised to do so again, so I wore my Gore-Tex pants and the Gore-Tex parka.

I left the motel about 8:15 and stopped in Denny's. The only one of the crew I talked to the day before who was there was Chris, the lady I talked to when I first went in. I think she's the hostess. I told her, "I woke up in the middle of the night and felt like I should come in here and tell you that I feel strongly that one of you — or maybe more than one of you — is thinking about doing something for the Lord, and I think you should just get off your butt and do it." I didn't intend that to be so abrupt, so I stammered a bit and said, "That's, uh, all I wanted to say."

Chris said, "Well, God bless you. Thanks for coming in. You be safe. And have a good trip."

So that's just what I did. I walked under the Interstate 75 bridge. There was a mist in the mountains there that reminded me of the Great Smokies, except this was 100% humidity — whoof! I walked 25 minutes or so — the mile and a half to just before a KOA campground. I stopped on the porch of the Valley Treasures Antiques and Collectibles, which is right across the street from the Keepsake Shop. Both stores were closed and the Valley Treasures shop wouldn't open until 10:00. So I sat there for a few minutes to see if the rain would stop.

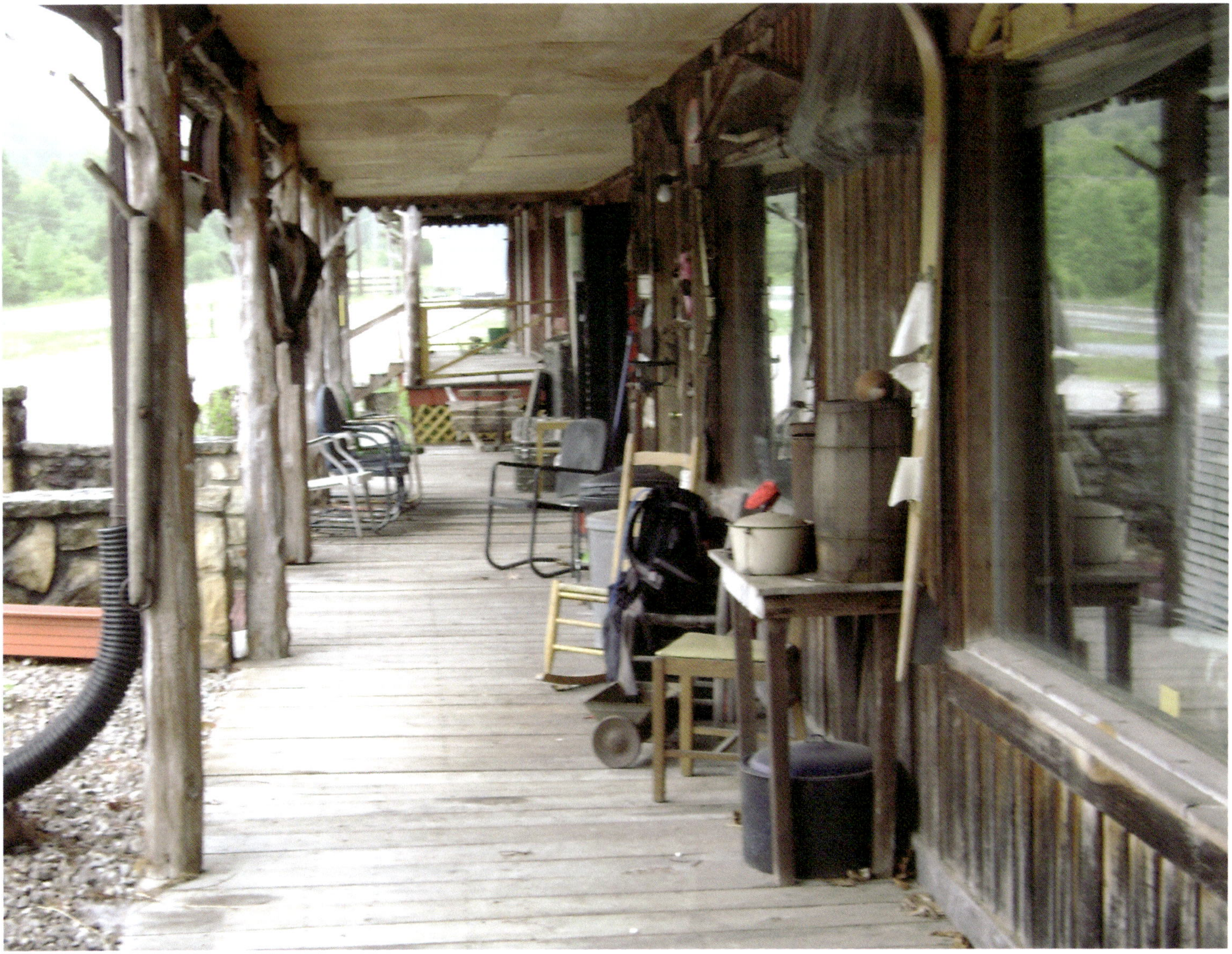

Out by the road, a sign for the Valley Treasures shop had a music staff with a four note motif repeated again and again. In addition to the drawings of a guitar and a fiddle, there are a couple of backward eighth notes floating around, just to keep you guessing. Renfro Valley is supposed to be Kentucky's answer to Nashville. Someone should talk with the folks who designed that sign.

It was raining pretty hard when I stopped. With my Gore-Tex pants and parka on I was pretty dry, but I was sweating like a pig.

Life was good. I thought I'd sit there for 10 or 15 minutes and then see if I could make it halfway to Berea. Berea is about 13 miles from Renfro Valley. If I could get six miles under my boots today, that would be enough, considering the condition of my feet — and the condition of the weather.

At 9:30 I decided to move on. It had finally stopped raining hard. It was still drizzling a bit, but it wasn't too bad. So, I put my parka back on and walked off the porch.

At 9:40 I went by the KOA which was supposedly a mile and a half from the exit back there. And just across the street from it I had to step over a rattlesnake that was pretty dead. The snake was about two feet long. I was sorry for the rattler, but happy I hadn't encountered it when it was alive.

20 minutes up the road from the antique shop I went past the Mt. Vernon city limits, and about a tenth of a mile past that I found the Christian Appalachian Project on Beiting Lane. I sat on their guard rail for a couple minutes and caught my breath, and then moved on.

Farther up the hill (All these hills felt like mountains to me!) I stopped at the Rockcastle County Adult Education Center. This was an old motel that they've turned into a bunch of offices.

They provide adult education classes, GED preparation, family literacy instruction, English as a second language classes, workforce education and reading instruction for eligible Kentuckians. It's affiliated with the Christian Appalachian Project that I had just walked by. I took off my backpack and sat at the picnic table next to the road in the shade of a beautiful tree. Candy Allen came out and asked if I needed anything.

I thanked her and told her about myself. About that time Keith Gilbertson[4] came out and introduced himself. Keith teaches computer science classes there. He offered to show me around. They had turned the original restaurant at the motel into a computer classroom. The rooms were used as offices and tiny classrooms. It seemed like a great way to get more use out of a building.

Keith said, "I'm going to go to lunch in a little while. Do you want to go with me?"

He offered to drive me to Renfro Valley. When I told him I didn't want to go back the way I came he told me that up the other way a couple of miles was a little place he drove by now and then but had never been in. He said the sign outside always seemed to have a letter or two missing or misplaced. What was being advertised was sometimes pretty mysterious.

While I waited for him, I sat on the picnic table under the tree by the road. I was sticky wet with sweat, but, you know, that was alright. The rain seemed to be stopping, so I took off the parka and rain pants, rolled them up, and stored them back in my backpack. By the time Keith was ready for lunch, some of the sweat had evaporated.

Snyder's Market and Café is a real throwback — much like the little places I remember from when I was a kid. You can buy anything from bait to groceries there. Why, they even have tanning beds! I loved the place!

Pinto beans didn't seem like a good idea. I had already learned that bathroom stops were not something to take for granted. I had a turkey and Swiss cheese sandwich on white bread and some chips. Keith had a BLT. Some canned A&W Root Beer helped wash it down. The food was plain but good.

The company was even better. Keith grew up in Minnesota and moved to Kentucky to work with the C.A.P. about 25 years ago. His twin sons graduated from M.I.T. One is now working at the Goddard Space Center and the other (I think I remember this right) is with Lockheed. He has another child who is a high school senior. We talked of our mutual admiration for the glorious scenery. He told me of his love for the outdoors and how easy it is for him here to just walk away from civilization. I thought that even at work, he was pretty far away from the hubbub compared to where I had lived in northern Virginia for 30 years.

We shared our concerns about the lack of trust in our society. People just don't trust anyone any more — from the White House to the folks next door. A little leadership would be appreciated. Finding that our elected representatives lie to us pretty regularly doesn't help instill confidence. As my friend Albert says, "A dead fish stinks from the head."

Keith mentioned the weapons of mass destruction that local people believe are stored just up the road near Richmond. I had never heard that particular conspiracy theory.

We agreed that the infotainment industry doesn't help. We are constantly bombarded with stories on whatever is gory and/or tawdry. As William Randolph Hearst said, "If it bleeds, it leads." When you hear depressing "news" all the time, you begin to believe that sort of thing typifies the society we live in.

On a lighter note, when I told him about my trip, I mentioned the rattlesnake I had seen earlier that day. He asked me if it was flat. I told him it was, indeed, pretty flat. He told me that people around there don't like rattlesnakes (or any snakes, I suppose) very much. They have learned that if a snake is big enough, when you run over it you may not kill it. So, when they see one on the road, just before they are going to hit it, they jam on the brakes so the car skids across it instead of rolling over it. That flattens the snake and makes sure it's pretty thoroughly dead.

Well... OK... It isn't a lighter note for local snakes.

When Keith left to go back to work I stayed for a while and talked to Sally, the owner of Snyder's. She's owned the place for five years. She said she worked with Keith, and then she worked for Toyota for a while before being able to buy Snyder's. She's kept it much like she found it, and likes it that way. I told her I liked it that way, too.

Leaving Snyder's about 1:15, the weather was absolutely beautiful! There were big, fluffy clouds up above. The rain had stopped. The humidity was down quite a lot and there was a little breeze. The sun, however, was hot. I thought I probably had about five miles to go to get to Berea. Once again, the estimate was about half of the reality.

By 3:00, the mailboxes had all been saying Berea for a while, so I had made it — at least to the outskirts of town. It took more than another hour, though, to get to the heart of town.

Eventually, I found myself on the porch in front of the VISTA office about 4:00. I asked the fellow sitting there if, by chance, they had a Coke machine inside. It turned out they didn't have even a drinking fountain. They did, however have Debra Collett-Blansett. She works there and took an interest in what I was doing. I asked her how far it was to the heart of town. She said she was driving right through there and would drop me off. It was only about a mile. My feet were aching again, so I took her up on it.

She told me of how her religious beliefs differed from those of most Christians and told me of the visions she had had. When we had traveled that last mile we were right in the middle of Berea College. I thanked her for the ride.

In researching schools for some of the young people in Sneedville I had heard that Berea College provides college educations for Appalachian children. I decided to see if I could get some information that might help the kids at Sneedville.

On campus I asked someone walking toward me for directions to the Admissions Office. His name was Wayne Messer, and he and I talked about favorite authors and all sorts of things. We talked so long I hope I didn't make him late.

I told Laura Sands[5], one of the people in the Admissions Office, about my walk and about the Sneedville mission. She introduced me to Chuck Morgan, Associate Director of Admissions. He was kind enough to talk with me for 10 or 15 minutes. The college actually has an Associate Director of Admissions for Berea in Hancock County, Mr. Lynn Murphree. According to Mr. Morgan, Berea is actively trying to get students from Hancock County. He said he thought some had attended in the past. He didn't indicate there were any currently....

I asked Mr. Morgan where I should spend the night. He told me Berea College owns the Boone Tavern Inn and Restaurant which is just about a block away, across the street. There were other places, but they were a couple or three miles away, and I didn't think my feet would make a couple more miles. A block seemed to be more than enough.

So I hobbled over to the Boone Tavern Inn and Restaurant. It has been in continuous operation since 1909. Daniel, of course, has been dead since 1820. The room was awfully expensive. The food was just OK. But the iced tea was absolutely wonderful!

July 12th – July 15th
Berea to Richmond, Kentucky

    I left the Boone Tavern Inn Thursday morning, and walked out of Berea. My goal was to reach Richmond — about 15 miles. I wasn't in any hurry and wanted to take it easy on my feet.

    A few cotton-ball clouds floated overhead, but off in the distance, north and west of me, they seemed to be congregating, suggesting rain later in the day. There was a lovely, cool breeze, but once again, the sun was hot. The humidity was supposed to go way up later in the day, but in the morning, it wasn't bad. In fact, it was a gorgeous day!

    There hadn't been enough rain in the Midwest to keep the farmers happy. The word *drought* had even been bandied about. When I started out, not being a farmer, everything looked lush to me. But having talked to people who worked the land, I was learning to look at things differently. The crops that had been planted were coming up puny and stunted. The creeks and rivers I crossed ran sluggish and low in their banks. Problem indicators were there aplenty, but most city folk like me don't know what to look for. If it's green, things must be OK.

    Still, it all *looked* lovely....

I walked past the Hogg Plumbing, Electric and Hardware Shop. Doesn't that conjure up an image or two?

Around 11:00 or so I stopped by a mailbox that said Mr. Jack Manley lived there. I sat next to his driveway in the shade of a couple of trees. I had probably only walked about three miles. I had been walking at a pretty good clip with no stops, but now it was time to stop for a little bit.

I walked by Midway Auto Mart Classic Cars. There were all sorts of old cars there, including a 1955 Pontiac Starchief that looked to be in pretty good shape.

At a little after 12:00 I made it to the Midway Express Marathon gas station and mini mart at a big intersection at the top of a hill, and I was ready to take a break. I had a double cheeseburger and some A&W root beer and sat for a little while. About 1:00 I headed north again. It was still beautiful out.

Just before 2:00. I sat in front of 4016 Richmond Road for about half an hour or so. I took a little nap. About the time I was drifting off to sleep, the lady at 4016 came out and offered me a Pepsi. Wasn't that nice? I had just had two cans of A&W Root Beer, so I turned her down. But it was nice to have someone offer hospitality like that.

At 3:15 I stopped at the Madison Gardens Memorial Garden Cemetery driveway back by the second tree, and just ran out of gumption. So I thought I'd quit for a while. But at 3:20 some people pulled into the cemetery and the noise of their car woke me up. So I got up and walked some more. I hoped I would find someplace to get something to eat later.

Just before 4:00, I walked into the Little BP Food Mart at 1900 Berea Road. I had a big vanilla soft serve ice cream and a big iced tea, and I thought I was ready to walk the last two miles to the town, so at 4:30 I was on the road again.

On the east side of the road before getting to Richmond there's an eight-foot fence that runs for miles with three stands of barbed wire on the top on the east side of the road and signs that say:

> *U.S. Army*
> *Bluegrass Army Depot*
> *Keep Out!*

There were lots of freight cars inside up the hill and cows grazing on part of the property inside that fence. Maybe this is where Keith said there were biological weapons stored right off the road.

Around 5:20, I stopped by a bunch of hysterical markers. I was still a mile or two outside of Richmond. Regardless of what that guy said back at the BP station, I still had a ways to go.

There hadn't been any shade near the road for a long time, and I couldn't see any up the road. I needed to sit down for a while and get out of the sun. The Daniel Boone's Trail historical marker gave just enough shade to cool me down a bit, and as an added bonus it served as a backrest! I sat there for five or 10 minutes, and then moved on.

At 6:00, I walked into the Marathon Mini Mart across the street from Captain D's Seafood. They didn't have any place to sit down. So I sat on the curb. I had a container of Minute Maid Orange Juice in a cup full of ice, which cooled me down. I asked the lady inside how far it was to the nearest hotel and she said, "Oh… a mile and a half or two." That seems to be the standard answer for everything here. I didn't know how far I still had to go, but I was certain it was more than "… a mile and a half or two."

I finally got to the main intersection in town about 6:30. Route 25 turns to the right there. As I was crossing the street, a fellow in a pickup truck in the left turn lane rolled down his window and said, "I seen you walkin' a ways back. I was gonna pick you up, but couldn't get to the right lane. I had to do some shoppin' and when I come out, there you are! Want a ride?"

I asked him where I could find a Days Inn or a Holiday Inn or something and he said, "Does it have to be one of them? They're a couple miles up thataway." He pointed up Route 25 north. Then he said, "There's a pretty good place right down the road. It's a whole lot cheaper than those others." He was pointing to the west — not the way I had planned to go.

"Uh…" I began.

"C'mon," he said, "You'll have to jump in the back. The passenger seat is full of stuff. Get in. I'll take you there."

So... with my feet killing me, having walked about 12 miles, I crawled (jumping wasn't going to happen!) into the pickup bed. He drove me straight ahead (not taking the right to go up Route 25) to the cheap motel. Once again "... right down the road...." turned into about three miles. He helped me out of the pickup bed, and drove off.

I looked around and thought I was on a set from the movie *Deliverance*. It definitely didn't look like a bunch of people I wanted to spend the evening with. I walked into the office where I found a fellow sitting in the middle of stacks of paperwork and other stuff. He looked up from his little desk and asked, "D'ya want a room for a night, a week, or a month?"

"Uh..." I stammered, "How much is a night?"

"$26.95," he answered.

"Uh..." I began, "Do you take plastic?"

"Nah," he answered, "just cash."

Inwardly I sighed in relief, "I don't travel with cash," I said. And I thanked him and walked out. I felt like I had been reprieved.

Now, of course, I had to walk the three miles back to the intersection with Route 25. My feet weren't any too happy about that. When I got back there, I turned left and headed up Route 25.

A couple miles up the road there was not only no sign of a motel, but it looked like I was running out of town, too. I walked up to a guy who was waiting to turn south onto Route 25 and asked him where the nearest motel was.

"You're heading the right way," he said, "Just keep going another five miles or so."

Oh, great! Thanks to the fellow taking me to the Deliverance Hotel, I had already added five miles or so to my day. I figured I had walked about 17 miles and there just wasn't another five miles in me. I stood there for a minute, trying to decide what to do. I had just walked a couple miles from downtown and there weren't any hotels the way I had come. I could see a restaurant a long way back the way I had come. There wasn't any place to eat nearby — just some car dealerships. There wasn't any place where I thought I could sleep the night without the local sheriffs picking me up.

I was in a pickle.

I debated with myself for a long time before I decided to try to hitchhike for ten minutes and see what might happen. I stuck my thumb up. Bobby Russell[6], the driver of the third vehicle, stopped his pickup truck and gave me a ride. He said that though he used to thumb rides, now he never picks up hitchhikers, but something made him pick me up. I'm pretty sure he used the same words — that he "felt compelled" to pick me up. I do remember staring at him at the time.

Bobby drove me to the Days Inn, a couple of miles away. We stood around in the parking lot and talked after we arrived there.

He grew up in Richmond and said he went to church at the Red House United Methodist Church nearby. It was Thursday evening and once again my feet were failing me. I decided to stay in Richmond through the weekend. So I asked if he planned to go to church the next Sunday. He said he didn't go much any more. Perhaps he would go this week, he said, and if he did, he'd give me a ride.

The Days Inn didn't have a guest computer or laundry, and if I was going to stay the weekend I needed at least a washer and dryer. Friday morning I called the nearby La Quinta hotel. They said they had both a guest computer and laundry services. So I stuffed everything back in my backpack and hobbled a bit more than a mile over there.

I called Bobby Russell Saturday, but just got his answering machine. I left a message telling him I was going to go to Red House UMC Sunday. If I didn't hear from him, I would take a cab.

With a name like Red House UMC, I thought it would have to be an interesting place. Sunday morning I hadn't heard back from Bobby, so I called a cab. The driver took me way out in the country (about eight miles out of town) to Red House UMC. It's a lovely old building, dedicated in 1907 and registered on the Blue Grass Trust for Historic Preservation.

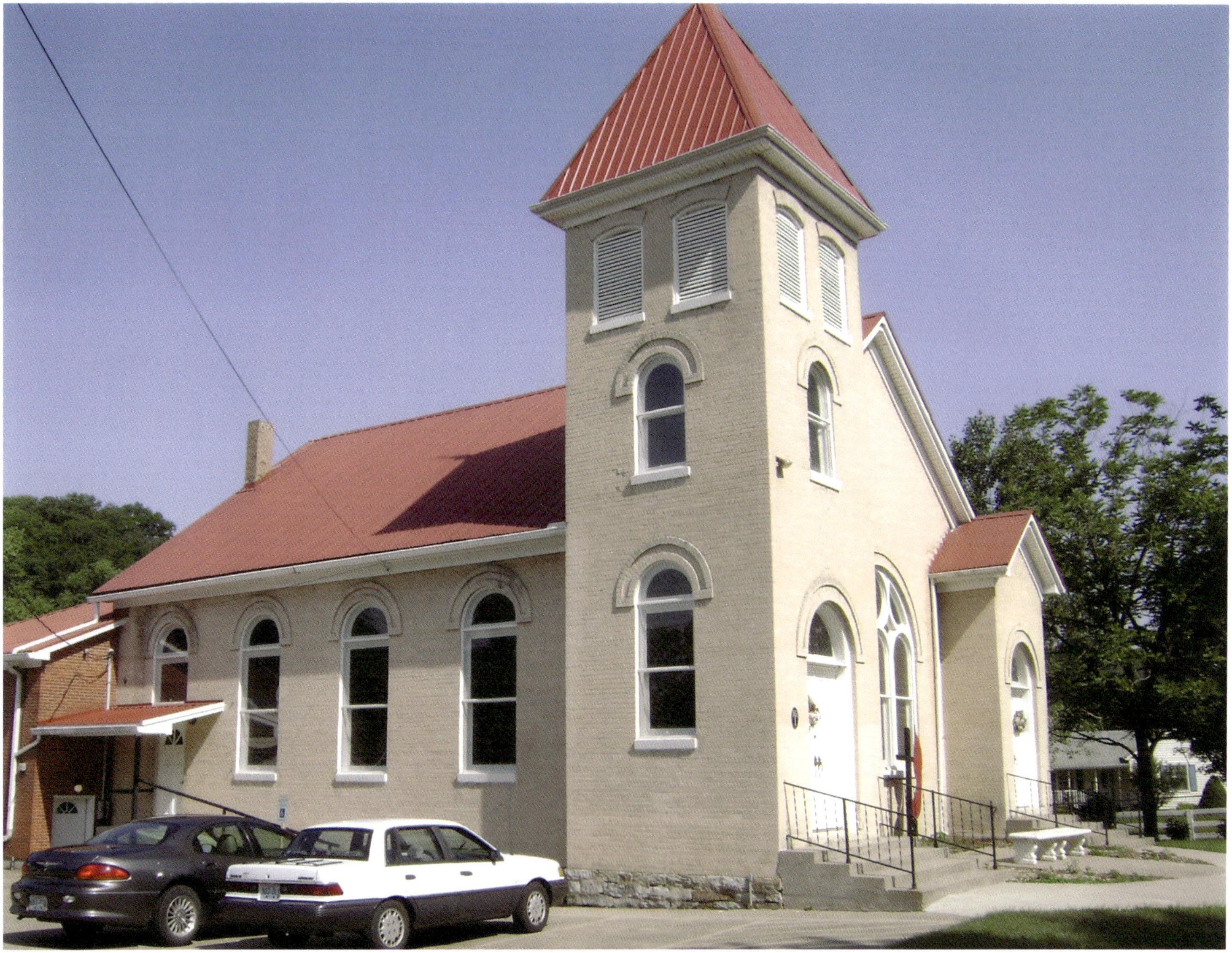

Patterned stained glass windows produced a soft, gentle atmosphere inside. The curved, wooden pews were not only beautiful, but comfortable as well. Their gentle curve echoed the arch of the ceiling which is finished in thin strips of darker wood. It's a beautiful room, lovingly kept up. I was disappointed to see a plethora of microphones and big speakers, however. In such a small space — a space with good acoustics — none of that should have been necessary.

The bulletin said 33 people attended last week. There were about 30 this day, July 15th.

Before the service, Ken Weitkamp introduced himself and his wife Mary. He asked if my last name was German. We talked about our shared German heritage before the service. Ken also introduced me to the pastor, Rev. Sam Knox. Sam is a retired pastor who just couldn't stop, it seems. When the previous pastor left Red House, Sam volunteered to step in and serve.

Before his sermon, Rev. Knox invited me to tell the congregation what I was doing. Then he preached on Genesis 22, the story of Abraham and Isaac. His was a powerful message of obedience and trust. Rev. Knox is an emotional speaker. Though his audience was small, there was complete attention while he spoke. I was deeply moved by him.

His sermon reminded me of the Judy Collins song, *The Story of Isaac*, which ran through my head for the rest of the day. It's a chilling rendition of the story with harpsichord accompaniment.

After the service, I took a picture of Ken and Sam.

Rena, whose last name I'm sorry to say I don't remember, played the piano with great enthusiasm, improvising accompaniments as she played. I haven't heard that kind of playing in a long time. It was enjoyable.

Afterward, Ken asked if he could take me to lunch. We went to the Wendy's near the La Quinta Inn. We talked a lot over lunch. Ken is fervent in his belief and his faith is strongly based on both the Old and the New Testament. I enjoyed talking with him about faith and his experiences farming in Kentucky as well as working in a tool and die company before he (semi) retired. His wife was busy planning a reception and birthday party for two of the members of the church so she didn't go to lunch with us.

I spent the rest of the day trying to figure out just what I was doing. I had been thinking about my "walk" a lot. I was 15 days out of Tennessee. Ten of those days I sat on my butt in various motels.

I had imagined that I would sleep under the stars or in shelters. Shelters didn't exist in the small towns in southwest Kentucky. And sheriffs, apparently, didn't want people sleeping on the streets.

I had thought that people would provide me with food, either inviting me into their homes or buying meals. Well, a couple people had, indeed, bought me meals, but no one had invited me into their homes. After walking in the sun for hours, sweating buckets, I couldn't really blame them. I had been pretty naive, it seemed.

So far, I had walked only about 75 miles. I had ridden about 150. What kind of "walk" was that?

Was I supposed to be learning something?
Was I supposed to be...
            ...inspired?
                ...humbled?
                      ...disgusted?
                          ...enlightened?
                              ...strengthened?

All I seemed to be getting was sore feet. Surely, that wasn't the purpose....

Maybe there wasn't a purpose. Maybe I had imagined the whole thing....

And every time I got to that point, I knew, **at least**, that wasn't true. In my mind's eye, I could still see the scene I had witnessed at Wally's church in Cleveland. I knew I had, at least, started out the way I was supposed to. (OK... except for the robe and sandals....)

It seemed that all the people who had picked me up had something to share with me that enriched me spiritually. And they all seemed to find spiritual strength from our meetings, too. So maybe the rides were part of the "walk."

If I hadn't accepted those rides, I wouldn't have had those conversations. I would have been the poorer for not knowing those people.

Wouldn't I?

On the other hand, perhaps I would have met people who would have meant even more to me....

Eventually, I came to believe I was doing the right thing.

Of course, don't we all generally believe we are doing the right thing?

I was still full of uncertainties. But, then, the unknowable is precisely that, isn't it? Perhaps it wasn't my responsibility to understand. Perhaps I was just supposed to experience.

I kept finding myself going around in circles.

And that's when I had to step out of the whirlpool.

I could stop the "walk" any time I wanted to. I could take a bus home or call someone to come pick me up. But that definitely didn't seem the right thing to do.

I decided to continue to walk whenever I could. As for the rest — that was beyond my comprehension. And out of my hands....

July 16th
Richmond to Lexington, Kentucky

Monday morning I soaked my feet one more time and put fresh Mole Skin around the blisters. I didn't leave Richmond until about 9:30 in the morning. I felt pretty good. I was determined not to walk more than an hour at a time. Sometimes I stopped after only thirty minutes or so. It seemed harder to find shade to rest in than before. I hoped this wasn't a trend....

I had noticed the prettiest blue wild flowers lining many stretches of the roads in this stretch of Kentucky. Born with two black thumbs, I have no idea what they are. I'm sure if they appeared in someone's garden back in civilization, they would be called weeds.

I went through another of those nasty stretches with guard rails on both sides of the road and almost no shoulders. I walked through that tenth of a mile real fast!

I stopped at Mr. T's Landscape and Garden, but didn't see anyone there with a lot of gold jewelry or a Mohawk. The clerk, however, said there was a McDonald's and some other fast food place a couple miles up the road. I walked about a mile from Mr. T's and sat for a while under a nice little tree with some shade on the east side of the road, right next to a development called Indigo Acres or Indigo Farms. The clouds were coming in, so I decided not to sit there too long. It was five minutes 'til noon.

About 1:30 I came to a Shell station that had a mini mart. They made me a sandwich, and I drank two cans of A&W Root Beer. I had been conserving the water in my backpack and still had plenty. When I left, I went by a hysterical marker that said Cassius M. Clay had lived nearby. Not the boxer who became Muhammad Ali, you understand, but the Abolitionist who lived from 1810 until 1903. As Casey Stengel would say, you can look him up.

About 2:30 I came to Shiloh Ministries Center of Gathering. The building looked like it belonged down at Camp Jubilee. I knocked on all the doors, but no one was there. The east side of the building

offered a little shade. The weather was getting pretty hot and humid, and I was getting pretty tired and sore, so I sat there for a while. I think the fellow who lives next door had gone down to Jonesville Road in Tennessee and bought the two yappy little dogs I had heard down there and brought them up to Kentucky. They yapped from the minute I walked over to the Center of Gathering. Eventually, I found a shady spot where they couldn't see me. They stopped barking so much, and I fell asleep.

By 5:30, I couldn't sit still any more. I had managed to nap off and on through the hottest part of the day. The temperature and humidity seemed to have dropped a little bit, so I set off again. It turns out the fellow with the yappy dogs had a sign out front that said he had "retired" daschunds. I wondered if they got little gold watches when they retired.

I estimated I was about halfway to Lexington. I came to a fork in the road. (Yogi Berra would have told me to take it.) A sign pointing to the small road to the left said "Tourist Attractions," but didn't say what they might be. There was no town name or any other indication of what I might find down that way. I wanted to believe there might be a restaurant and maybe even a hotel down there.

On the other hand, I could see a truck stop about a quarter mile away down the right fork on what appeared to be the main road, which crossed over the Interstate. I couldn't decide whether to take a little detour toward the "Tourist Attractions" or walk across the Interstate to the truck stop.

Just then, a fellow heading north pulled up across the road and asked if I wanted a ride. He was the third driver heading north that day who pulled over and hollered across the road to see if I wanted a ride. I had turned down the other two.

I asked him if he knew what was down the left fork. He told me there wasn't any place to eat there, or much of anything else, really. I told him if that were the case, I'd appreciate a lift to the truck stop — my feet were killing me (again!).

When I got into his car he said he was going up I-75 to the next exit where there were a bunch of restaurants and hotels, and offered to give me a ride up there, instead of just to the truck stop. I took him up on it. He is Bob Flynn, a staff writer and photographer for the *Jessamine Journal*. He had been a freelance writer, but decided he wanted a steady job.

He took me to Lexington. It was just a few minutes away by car, but I hated to think how long it would have taken me to walk — especially with my feet as bad as they were. He drove me to the nearest Holiday Inn just off the Interstate. Some NASCAR team pulled in as I was heading out of the lobby to my room.

As I walked by the restaurant I noticed a sign that, among other things, indicated guests had to wear shoes. I told the owner there wasn't much chance of me putting shoes back on after I got to my room. After a little negotiation, we compromised on my thick, wool socks. I assured her they would pass for shoes unless they were examined closely.

After I got into the room and took off my boots, I went down and had dinner. The owner and the waitress both studiously avoided looking at my feet. I ate catfish there and it was excellent! The waitress's name was Zorka. She had a little accent and told me she was from Bulgaria. Her mother was knitting socks at a table by the kitchen door. Zorka was interested in what I was doing. We didn't get to talk too much because she was the only waitress in the restaurant and was very busy.

After dinner, I went back up to my room, soaked my aching feet, and slept like a log.

July 17th
Lexington, Kentucky

Bob Flynn had indicated that we were just south of Lexington. I figured I'd make it downtown, but that day I got the latest start so far. It was 9:50 when I left the Holiday Inn. I turned left at the end of the driveway and headed into town. I had decided maybe two pairs of socks were putting too much pressure on my feet, so after I soaked them again and put on fresh Mole Skin, I only wore one pair. In retrospect, that was a big mistake.

The fellow at the Holiday Inn desk said it was about four miles into town, and 12 miles through town, which is a whole lot more than I was told the night before. Sure enough though, as soon as the hotel guy told me four miles, I crossed the Interstate, walked about a half a mile and saw a sign that said "Lexington 8." Hah! So much, again, for distance measurements!

Fortunately, the weather was beautiful. There were some puffy clouds off at the horizon, but overhead the sky was a clear light blue. It promised to be another wonderful day to walk.

At about 11:10 I stopped under some trees at the top of a big hill near Ashley Woods Road. Some ducks retreated behind an expensive-looking fence. There were a couple of Palomino horses there, too. I had to take pictures of them for Viola, my youngest granddaughter. She's a regular cowgirl! The property looked like the sort of place you would expect in bluegrass country. But up close — at least near the fence — the grass was sort of thin. Maybe the horses liked to stand close to the fence so they could watch the cars — and the occasional walker — go by.

By now, the puffy clouds had begun to flatten out and roll overhead. Occasionally, it would drizzle a little, but not enough to seriously consider putting on my rain gear.

About 12:30 I stopped at the Lake Ellerslie Fishing Club entrance and sat under some trees by their driveway while a little rainstorm blew through. The leaves were thick enough that I didn't get wet. And I needed the rest.

A little after 1:00 I reached the Texas Roadhouse Restaurant. Although I hadn't seen a sign saying I was actually in Lexington, there were shopping centers and stores and the like. I could see 10- or 12-story tall buildings way off to the north, which I figured must be downtown.

About 3:00 I started up the road again. The waitress said there wasn't anything except a Double Tree Suites place nearby. I'd have to go all the way downtown (a mile or two, of course) and then go out Newtown Road (another mile or two — hah!) to where all the hotels were. I thought the Double Tree Suites would be a little pricey. Perhaps I could find something more economical where there was competition nearby.

About a half hour later, the rain came again, and this time it was pretty heavy. I ducked into a Bob Evans restaurant and had a piece of pie while it rained itself out. I hadn't had an excuse that good in a long time.

By now, it was 3:25 and my feet were killing me — again! The length of time I could walk and not be in pain was getting shorter and shorter, it seemed.

Lexington had public transportation, and a bus seemed like a good idea. I waited for about a half hour until it arrived on its way downtown. At the central terminal, I asked the dispatcher which bus I should take to get to a motel. Inside the bullet-proof glass booth where she sat, she conferred with another dispatcher and a policeman. There didn't seem to be any general agreement. Eventually, she told me I should try going out Newtown Road to the east of town. The instructions they gave me involved multiple buses and transfers. Due to my lousy hearing, much of what she said was unintelligible through the tinny little speaker.

Instead, I walked a couple blocks to the main intersection downtown. A bus went by labeled Georgetown Pike. That rang bells for me. Monday, Bob Flynn had told me about a Georgetown Baptist College or University that reached out to Appalachian children. So I walked up to the next bus stop and waited for the next Georgetown Pike bus.

The buses are about a half hour apart, but eventually a little one came along marked Georgetown Pike. It was a small bus with about 12 seats. The back was empty except for places to secure wheelchairs. The bus was pretty full. The driver and one of the women passengers were having a spirited argument about why it was better to live in Kentucky than in Mississippi. There was a lot of laughing and posturing and carrying on. It was a hoot!

We went by Transylvania University in the middle of town, but I didn't see any Georgetown College or University.

When most of the women had left, the driver (VW was the name on his name tag.) asked where I was going. He offered to give me a transfer to take me to a motel. After considering my options, he told me I'd be better off going back to the terminal. He said when we got there he would walk me over to the correct bus. And that's just what he did. In fact, he told the other driver to take me to the Holiday Inn and get me as close to the entrance as he could. Thank heaven for VW!

A half hour later — about 6:00 — I was there. This Holiday Inn is an enormous motel, and not inexpensive. In fact, I could probably have stayed at the Double Tree for the same amount of money. But my feet were pretty much toasted, and I didn't like the thought of trying to walk to someplace else, so I took a room. It felt wonderful to take off those boots!

July 18th
Lexington, Kentucky to West Chester, Ohio

At 9:25 on Wednesday, the 18th I was back on the road. The desk clerk at the hotel provided me with a map. It looked like the hotel was only a couple miles from Route 25. I started back down Newtown Road, walking past the rush hour traffic, and then I thought, "I don't want to go basically south back into town. But if I walk just a couple miles north on I-75, I'll get to where U.S. 25 crosses over." That would save a lot of time as well as a lot of walking.

Of course, it's not very legal to walk on Interstates. But I thought that if I were facing traffic, maybe the troopers would ignore me. As it turned out, I didn't see any troopers.

After an hour or so, I took a break and sat under the first bridge over I-75/I-64 where the two run together for a little ways. It was just before the ramp that takes I-75 north off the combined road. My feet were already hurting, and I don't think I had walked even two miles.

I rested for five or ten minutes, then crossed southbound I-75 (and eastbound I-64). I wasn't too happy about walking with traffic, but the alternative was a long, curving ramp, complete with hill and overpass. My feet told me to take the chance. There wasn't much of a shoulder on the left side of the road, so I crossed over to the right side.

About halfway around the ramp to where both directions of I-75 were next to each other again, there was an 18-wheeler parked on the shoulder. I hobbled up to it and tip-toed around the right side of the rig. I definitely wasn't going to put myself between the truck and the traffic going by on its left. On the right, however, there wasn't much more than a foot or two of flat shoulder before the ground sloped steeply down several feet into the ditch. As I inched past the big trailer and came next to the cab, the driver leaned out the passenger window and said, "You look kinda tired. Want a lift?"

"Well..." I stammered, "Uh...."

"Come on," he said, "I seen you walkin' back there. You look like your feet are killing you."

"They *are* killing me," I said. I had never been in an 18-wheeler, and having experienced people's inability to estimate distance over the last couple of weeks, I had little faith that I would come to U.S. 25 soon. So... I got in the truck.

C.D. Trog is a driver for Jet Express. He also does independent contract driving. He told me he's 50 years old and learned to drive a truck while he was serving time in the Army. He also worked as a cook and did other things as well. He managed to get out of the Army without getting into too much trouble. Now, when I say he "served time in the Army," that's exactly what he told me. He got into trouble with the law at a young age and the judge gave him the choice of going to jail or joining the Army. "He thought he was sending my sorry butt to Vietnam, but I never left Fort Jackson," C.D. said. Well, actually, he said it a lot more colorfully than that, but I'll clean up his language here. He said after doing all sorts of other stuff for most of his life, he's been driving a truck for the last three years or so. He's married to a woman down in Georgia, he said, but normally stays with his daughter in Dayton.

After seeing me hobbling along, C.D. decided I just didn't need to be walking any more. I think he might have had another motive. He told me he was finishing up 1,400 miles of driving in three days. My guess is, in addition to the humanitarian thoughts about my well-being, he was tired and wanted some company for the last couple hours it would take to get to Dayton.

"How far are you going?" he asked.

"Well..." I answered, "...to Michigan, actually. But I just want to get up to the next place where U.S. 25 crosses over I-75."

"Well, I'm going to Dayton," he said, "Why don't you let me drive you up there?"

"Actually," I said, "I'm supposed to meet some people in Cincinnati." Miriam Downey from First United Methodist Church in Kalamazoo had sent me an EMail telling me that her sister Sue attends Faith Community United Methodist Church in West Chester, Ohio — just north of Cincinnati and right off I-75. I thought I might be able to attend church there and meet Sue and her husband Kyle Jones.

"Well then," C.D. said, "I'll drop you in Cincinnati."

"Uh... Well... Uh... OK." I said. So, I let him.

We exchanged Army stories. He said he never put up with authority very well. He boxed for a while in the Army and as a civilian after he got out. He said he still likes to get into fights — just not as often as when he was younger.

C.D. talked and talked. I'll leave most of it out, but he told me he had ridden motorcycles since he was old enough to balance on the gas tank in front of his father. His father bought a new BMW motorcycle in 1968. I told him my friend Wally had a BMW motorcycle when we were in Ethiopia in 1968 — 1969. C.D. bought his dad's bike years ago. A few years ago, riding it at 60 MPH, he was in a head-on collision. He said he only broke his wrist and sanded a tattoo off his back, but it took his wife 18 months to learn how to walk again!

She's his second wife. He showed me her picture that he keeps on the visor of the truck. I can see why he married her, but wonder why she married him. He said he told her, "You're a smart, good-looking woman. You don't need to be doing what you're doing. You just need a good man to take care of you."

When her son was 17 a while back he had threatened C.D. C.D. told him that he had four sons, all of them a lot bigger than C.D., and they wouldn't even think of doing what the kid was thinking of. "I told him to go back to his room," C.D. said. And that's just what he did.

C.D. said to me, "You can't come between a woman and her son." I told him I knew that for a fact. When her son graduates from high school next year, C.D. plans on moving back in with his wife.

After the motorcycle wreck, C.D.'s insurance company offered him $400 or $500 for what was left of the bike. He fought with them over it and eventually they rebuilt it for him. He still rides it. In fact, he had just come back from North Carolina where he and his wife went hang gliding. No timid fellow, that. Nor, it appears, is his wife....

Just before he let me off after telling me about one of his close calls, C.D. said, "Yeah. You know. If it doesn't kill me, it makes me stronger."

"Yeah…" I said, "Nietzsche."

He said, "What?"

I said, "Nietzsche."

He said, "What's that?"

"The German Philosopher," I answered, "He said, 'That which doesn't kill me makes me stronger.'"

"Oh…" C.D. said, "Never heard of him." His timing was so perfect, I almost expected to hear a drum roll.

A little later C.D. said, "You know, I've been through some tight scrapes in my life, but I figure, you know, if you believe in God, or, you know, the universal spirit, or whatever you believe in, He'll never give you anything to do that He doesn't give you strength to find your way through it."

I looked at this guy who's about as earthy a person you can imagine — truck driver, tattooed all over, teeth out, dirty language, and everything else — and felt that his heart's in the right place. Well… I don't know… Mostly, it's in the right place. Hah hah hah! *I* liked him, anyway.

After a lot of stop and go traffic caused by an accident up ahead, C.D. let me out at the Tylersville Road exit, just north of Cincinnati. I hobbled up the ramp and into a Bob Evans Restaurant. After dinner I called Faith Community UMC and spoke with Gayla, the church secretary, who told me how to get there. She said I could see Cox Road from the front door of Bob Evans and it's only about a half mile from Tylersville Road. Of course, it was at least a mile. Once again, the distance estimate went awry. I guess we spend so much time in our cars and so little time walking that we aren't able to accurately estimate distance. We tend to think, instead, of how long it takes to drive somewhere. The translation to distance just doesn't work well.

When I got to the church, I met the pastor, Rev. David Bridgman. I told him what I was doing, and he said, "Well, you know… Sue and Kyle are not here. They're up in northern Michigan at their vacation place for the summer. But we'd love to have you for Sunday…."

Later, I went back and looked at Miriam's Email and, sure enough, she had said that Kyle and Sue were in Michigan, but that the church might be a good resource, if I ran into trouble. Apparently, my feet weren't the only parts of me that weren't in optimal working order. They were pretty bad, though. I decided to get off them for the rest of the week and give them another chance to get better.

I told Rev. Bridgman I had walked by an Econo Lodge coming over to the church, and asked if that would be a good place to stay. He and Gayla looked at each other and he said, "Noooo… You probably don't want to stay there." They talked a little bit, and decided I'd be best off at the Holiday Inn Express which is one exit south down I-75.

Rev. Bridgman said, "Well, I'm going down to the library which is just past there. I'll just take you right over, if you'd like." So he did.

When I was checking in and told Ashley Sulfsted[7], the clerk at the hotel, that I wanted to stay through Sunday night, I realized that would be five nights. That's a lot of nights and a lot of money, but I just couldn't imagine walking any more for a while.

Deidra Marshall, the Director of Human Resources for Holiday Inn in the area, was working with this hotel for a while. Holiday Inn had just purchased it, according to Deidra, and she was there to make certain the turnover was going well. She said, "Well... we've only got a smoking room tonight and a non-smoking room tomorrow night. And... I don't know. After that we've got nothing." I asked her if they could move me into something else in case somebody cancelled out. I spent the first night in the smoking room, but the last guests who used it must not have smoked much. It wasn't bad. The next morning they moved me into a non-smoking room. And someone did, indeed, cancel out, so I had a room through Sunday.

Deidra has a lovely contralto voice. I asked her if she sang, and she said, "Nope. You don't want to hear me sing."

I thought of Ted Voorhees, my friend from college days who became an Episcopalian Priest. He's about six feet four and has a voice like James Earl Jones. I served as cantor for him at All Saints Episcopal Church in Alexandria, Virginia long ago. Ted couldn't carry a tune, either. I told him I'd try to teach him, but he was convinced it was impossible and that, in fact, a lot of people with really resonant speaking voices couldn't sing. Since he told me his theory, I have been surprised at how many people with beautiful speaking voices have told me they can't sing.

So, anyway, there I was, just north of Cincinnati. I had to wait about 45 minutes before they got the room cleaned up. When I got to the room, I took my boots off and planned to leave them off except when I absolutely had to put them on. My feet **hurt**. Maybe just one pair of socks was not a good idea.

Wanda Hogan works, among other things, serving the Continental breakfast at the Holiday Inn. July 19th was her son's 17th birthday. She told me she has seven children — four of them adopted. I congratulated her. She said she was just trying to keep up with her grandmother, who adopted 31! Wow! Wanda is such a friendly person. I think she virtually adopts everyone who stays at the hotel. Unfortunately, she never stopped long enough for me to take her picture!

Wanda's friend, Jenny Dininger[8], was in the hotel Thursday morning. Jenny is a Registered Nurse, and Wanda asked her to take a look at my feet. "Nice blisters!" Jenny said. I don't think she meant it as a compliment. Jenny told me it would be a good idea to stay off them for a couple days.

She said I should use foot powder, keep them dry and wear two pair of socks when I wore my boots. She also recommended using Mole Skin around the blistered areas, and told me not to cut what appeared to be dead skin off them until the blister itself had cracked open. I think I've cut enough blisters off my feet in the last few weeks to make a coin purse.

I had called my son, Josh, the night before and asked him to do a little research on the Web concerning the blisters. He had given me almost the exact same information that Jenny did. So, now I had the same answer from two people on whether to wear one pair of socks or two, and I felt a bit better about spending five days sitting on my butt.

On Friday, the 20th, I walked about a half mile over to the WalMart to have a prescription refilled. On the corner of the WalMart center is a National City Bank branch. I didn't travel with much money, but that morning, I was pretty low. So I stopped in to use my debit card. I talked with Andrew Bowley[9], the teller, for a while until I noticed someone was waiting behind me.

I walked across the parking lot to the WalMart store. In addition to the prescription, I also bought some baby powder (the pharmacist said that as long as I didn't have anything but blisters, I didn't need medicated foot powder), some more Mole Skin and Mole Foam, and some other stuff. I had lunch at the Subway there. While he was making my sandwich, Clint[10] and I talked about what I was doing.

At home I never shop at WalMart. But often there was one right on the road where I was walking, and they had all the things I needed. Practicality (along with trying to rest my feet) won out over my sense of social consciousness, I guess.

As soon as I got back to the hotel, I took off my boots, soaked my feet, and put them up. There's only so much sitting still I can do, though — as I found out the year before, after the surgeries. And I really don't like television. I'm afraid I was just about bored senseless.

I was following the medical advice I had, but again I had doubts about whether I was doing the right thing. I couldn't believe one of the objects of this "Walk" was supposed to be for me to wreck my feet. But then again, how was I to know what I was supposed to be doing? The vision didn't come with an instruction book, and other than what I saw and the deep feeling I had that I was supposed to walk out of Camp Jubilee, I was on my own.

In my naivete, I had thought I would stay in homeless shelters and eat at soup kitchens on days when no one offered to take me into their homes for dinner or a place to sleep. Silly me. I hadn't found much evidence of social services to help the homeless in the little towns I had passed through. Or the big ones, for that matter!

I was fortunate enough to be able to eat in restaurants and sleep in hotels (when I could find them). It occurred to me that if I had found shelters and soup kitchens to take advantage of, I would have been using resources that someone in dire straits wouldn't be able to use. That line of reasoning made staying in hotels and eating at restaurants more acceptable. Of course, the clean sheets and better food didn't hurt....

The only amenity I needed that the Holiday Inn didn't have was a coin-operated laundry. Friday, I asked where the nearest one was. Neither Deidra nor Ashley knew of one nearby. They said they'd think about it. Saturday, I asked to borrow a Yellow Pages to see if I could find one. Deidra went in the back to find a Yellow Pages. When she came out she asked, "Why don't you let us do your laundry for you?" It didn't take much convincing to get me to agree. I didn't know how I was going to get to a laundry and back. I hadn't seen one at the WalMart shopping center, and that meant a long, long walk. I was so grateful to them.

Sunday morning I called the West Chester Taxi Service at 9:55. They told me they'd have a taxi at the hotel in 15 or 20 minutes. I thought that would give me plenty of time to get to Faith Community UMC. At 10:20 I called again. The dispatcher assured me the driver was on the way. At 10:40 I called again — same promise. At 10:50 I called and got the driver. He assured me he was only five minutes away. He arrived at the hotel at 11:00. I arrived at the church at 11:10. I didn't miss much, I guess, but the waiting was frustrating.

Rev. Bridgman preached. He spoke about Samuel and Saul and David. Quoting John Ortberg[11], he told us to, "Ruthlessly eliminate hurry." Needless to say, I identified very strongly with that — particularly after sitting on my butt, resting my feet. Great stuff!

After the service I took some pictures of the sanctuary and went to the chancel to look around. They had a grand piano and an organ and another keyboard. The Christian Living Center down the hall held a contemporary worship service on Sundays, and functioned as a basketball court, among other things, on other days.

Big LC screens and a circular, art deco stained glass window over the sanctuary entrance add color, but to my eye — accustomed to the textures and colors in the Late English Gothic cathedral I attend in Kalamazoo (see the picture, on the next page) — it all looked sort of pale. Perhaps the designers planned for the color and texture to come from the parishioners.

In the sanctuary, I met Dave Elvy, who was talking with Susan Little. Susan played the piano and organ and sang a solo during the service. Dave invited me to lunch, and I accepted. He works for a company that prepares MREs and similar commercially-available food products. He is in the process of going back to college, but this has caused him to have to sacrifice directing the men's choir at the church. He's still active in music there, though not as much as before.

Dave and I had similar opinions about the info-tainment industry and its constant droning negativism. We shared stories about music experiences and our faith journeys. It was a very fulfilling time. Afterward, Dave dropped me back at the Holiday Inn.

So there I was, getting ready to walk again the next day. The worst thing about sitting there the last couple of days was that the weather had been absolutely glorious. Sunny and cool with nice breezes — just the sort or weather I should have been walking in. It would be nice if that trend continued.

I was just about halfway home, with a little less than 300 miles to go. At the rate I was going, I might be back before October.

July 23rd
West Chester to Hamilton, Ohio

At breakfast, I met Larry G.[12] from Carmel, Indiana. He and his wife had been attending a Little League tournament and were returning home. I had been saying goodbye to Wanda, and he joined our conversation for a bit.

Then, I left the Holiday Inn Express and walked down to a Marathon station where Cincinnati-Dayton Road crosses Tylersville Road. The clerk at the Dunkin' Donuts inside said that I'd probably like walking on Tylersville Road better than the going down Route 129. So, I headed west up Tylersville Road.

Tylersville Road is a pleasant walk. There are a lot of houses, but no sidewalks or shoulders. So I walked across people's front yards. Sometimes the footing was pretty uneven. I am still cautious about my left ankle, which is weak from the injury I had when I was a kid.

About 10:30 I stopped at St. Anne's Episcopal Church to rest for a little bit and give my blisters time to recuperate. I kept staring at the church sign. I haven't seen Ted Voorhees in twenty-some years. We were at Methodist College years ago, and he went on to become an Episcopal priest. The last I heard, he was in western Ohio somewhere. I decided to go in and ask if anyone there knew how I could contact Ted.

The pastor, Jeff Bunke, and I talked for close to half an hour. He knew Ted, but hadn't seen him in several years. He found Ted's name and a phone number on line and gave them to me. He offered to buy me lunch, but he was going east and I was going west, so I turned him down. A little after 11:00 I headed west again.

A couple miles after I left the church I was walking on the right shoulder when a blue van in the westbound lane pulled over. The driver hollered across the road, "Do you want a ride?"

I said, "No. Not really," but he just sat there, so I walked over to talk to him.

He said, "I'm the guy who took you over to church yesterday."

I looked at him and said, "Oh...?"

He said, "I shaved my beard."

"Well, yes you did," I said, "Look at that!" The car he used in his taxi business was a Chrysler minivan and it didn't have any sign to indicate it was a taxi.

"Come on. Get in," he said, "There's somebody I want you to meet."

As he drove, he told me a lot about Rev. Kenny Mills. Carl said when Kenny was young he would get in a fight at the drop of a hat — and he always won. I asked him what turned Kenny around. Carl said he didn't know. He figured he must have just got right somehow.

Carl said Kenny ran an outreach mission to drug addicts and other forgotten souls out of his little church. So I got in the van, and he drove me to Hamilton, Ohio, which is where I was headed anyway.

Carl took me to Mills Moving and Storage or Tri-County Moving and Storage, depending on which part of the sign you were looking at. He took me inside to find Kenny, but Kenny wasn't there when I arrived. Carl introduced me to Kenny's associate, Rev. Carl Stewart. I asked Rev. Stewart where I could get lunch. Both Carls agreed that Brewer's Coffee Shop just down the street would do nicely.

Kenny arrived before I left, and we talked for a while. He asked how I was, and I told him that, except for the blisters, I was doing just fine. When I asked how he was, he said, "I feel **good**! Yeah! I feel so good, I can put a couple bobcats in a couple burlap bags, swing 'em over my shoulder, walk a mile on a bob-wire fence, and spit in the eye of a puma!"

"You must be feeling pretty good, then," I replied.

Among other things, Kenny said when he was about 20 years old he was baptizing a girl and he started speaking in a foreign language he didn't understand. And he's been speaking in tongues and preaching ever since.

After a while, I walked two blocks north to Brewer's Coffee Shop for lunch. I didn't see a whole lot of coffee happening there. The place was a good little restaurant, though. I walked in just before noon and had a steak burger and some fries and some iced tea.

By the time I got to the middle of town, it was after 1:00, and my feet were hurting. I came to the bridge over the Ohio River and there was a welcome center. I walked in and asked the ladies there where I could stay. One of them said, "The only hotel in town is closed for renovation, but there's a bed and breakfast across the river. If you turn left on B Street, you'll be right there."

So I did. And, sure enough, The Roseville Inn, owned and operated by Bill and Jackie Groth, put me up for the night. It was lovely. Bill is an investment counselor and does sessions in Kalamazoo now and again. He said it's just about exactly 250 miles up to Kalamazoo from Hamilton. They have a standard poodle named Marley. They named him after Bob Marley because of his tightly curled brown hair. What a hoot!

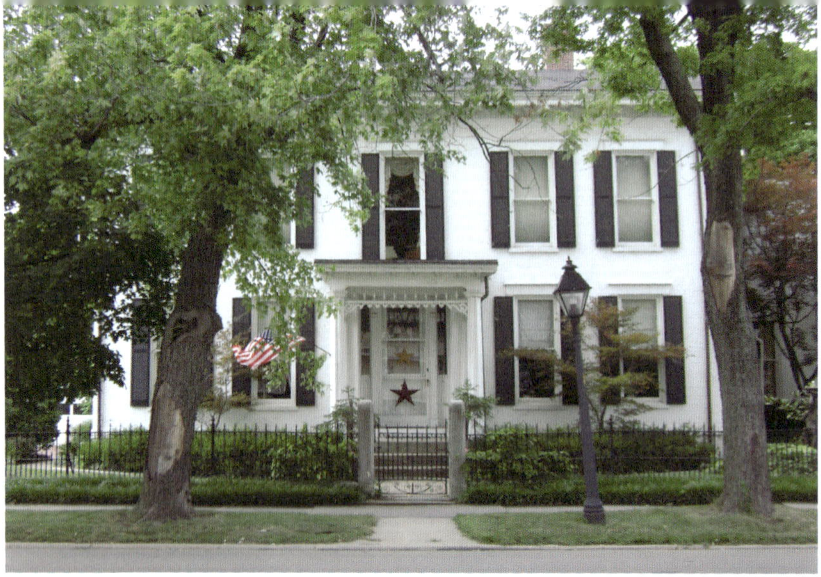

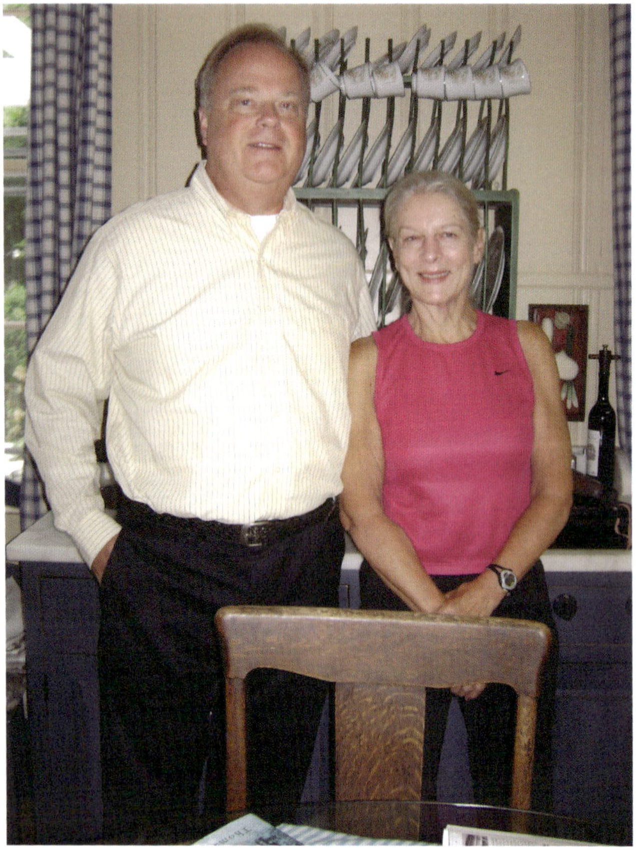

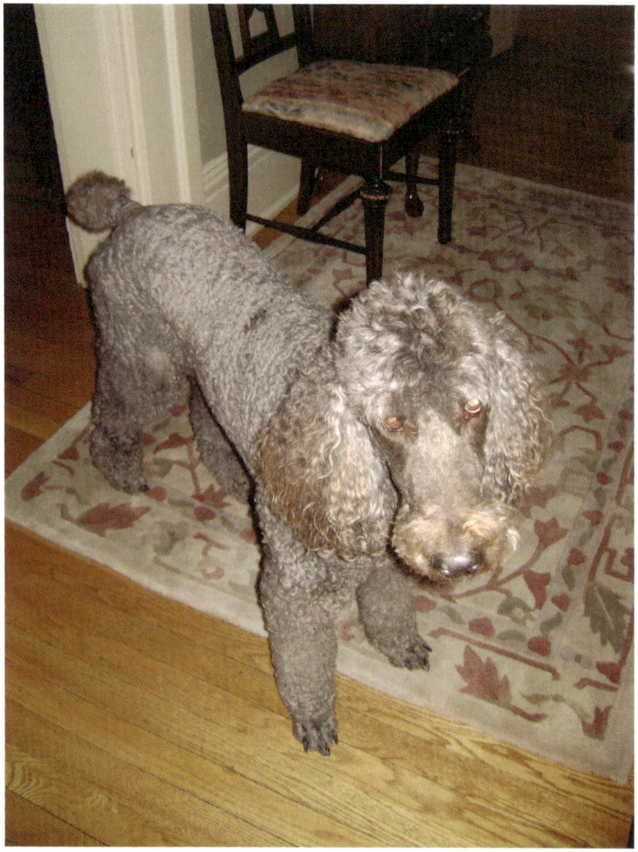

July 24th
Hamilton to Oxford, Ohio

At 8:20 on Tuesday morning, I was walking again toward Richmond, Indiana. Coming out of Hamilton, there was a time/temperature sign that said 73 degrees. There was a little breeze, and it was overcast and cool — a gorgeous day for walking.

About 10:50, I came to Jesse Drive where there are four trees in front of somebody's house. I sat down to take a five minute break, but I didn't get up until 11:30. It was so comfortable under those trees. Except for getting ants all over me, I had a nice nap. The rain was holding off. I hoped that trend would continue.

A couple hours later I walked by the Carl Dozier Memorial Park, given by the National Association of Letter Carriers. I wondered who Carl Dozier was, but didn't see a sign or anything. Just past the park, some bozo passing someone on Route 177 going west came from behind me and went by my right side with about a foot to spare while I was walking on the shoulder there. That probably took a year off my life!

At 1:35 I arrived at Darrtown, Ohio. There's a stone marker in a little park off the road that says Darrtown was the home of Walter (Smokey) Alston. From a little town that is about four blocks square, he went a long way.

The only place in town that had anything to eat was Bob's Carryout. After I had a sandwich I walked a couple blocks to the Darrtown United Methodist Church to see if I could sleep there. There wasn't anybody at the church. I could see the Baptist Church across the street, and there wasn't anybody there either. It was Tuesday afternoon, after all, at 2:20. So I sat on the front porch of the church, took my shoes and socks off and let my feet air out. I had walked more than eight miles and my feet were sore. I decided I wasn't going any farther today.

The Methodist Church has a large, covered, concrete porch. It would provide shade and keep me dry in the rain that appeared to be on the way. I dozed off and on while I waited for someone to come and tell me it was alright for me to stay there. Or that it wasn't. I didn't see many people over the next several hours — one couple out for a walk, a few cars, and one lady out mowing her lawn. The walkers waved. Those in cars didn't seem to notice me at all. A couple across the street, packing away their travel trailer, seemed to glare at me occasionally while they were working, but they went inside without coming over to find out what I was doing..

About 7:00, I went over to Bob's and bought a pizza and a bottle of water. I went back to the church and ate it all. I was just putting another piece of MoleSkin on my right heel when a lady walked up and asked what I was doing. I told her about my journey and said I'd like to sleep on the church porch. It turned out she was a member of the church. She said, "That sounds OK to me."

After the woman left, somebody drove by heading over to Bob's with a car stereo full of really nasty rap music. I could hear the four-letter words from a block and a half away. And it occurred to me it was like a bubble of hate floating through the world... a bubble of hate....

At 9:00 as I was getting ready to go to sleep on the porch, a gentleman named Ken Russell rode up on a bicycle. We talked for a while. He's a member of the church, too, and he said, "No. I think it's just fine. If you want to sleep here I don't think there's any problem." He said they used to leave the front door of the church open and sometimes people would come in and sleep on pews. They stopped doing that for fear of vandalism.

We were sitting there trading Army stories and stuff like that, and up drove a sheriff from Butler County. He called in to check my ID, and said, "Well, if this guy says you can sleep here, I guess you can..." Then he said, "But we don't recommend it. I'd sooner you didn't."

I said, "Well..."

"You know," he said, "some people come home late at night and they've been drinking, and I'm liable to have to take you to the hospital instead of, you know, instead of taking you to a hotel or something."

"Well..." I said, "I don't want to cause any trouble. If there's a hotel nearby, take me to a hotel and I'll go stay in a hotel."

Mr. Russell didn't offer to let me stay at his house, so Sheriff Mike Barger took me to Oxford, home of Miami University of Ohio, and dropped me at the hotel. I walked in to the Hampton Inn & Suites and the girl behind the counter asked, "Are you checking in?"

"Well, uh..." I said, "Actually I'm looking for a room. Do you have any vacancies?"

"Oh, no," she said, "we're booked."

"Oh," I said, "Well... where's the nearest other hotel?"

She said, "Well, if you walk out the door and turn right, it's about a block down the street."

Now, I know all about "…a block down the street," becoming two, three, or more. So that didn't make me too happy. My feet were not good. As I was putting my backpack on, the girl said to the guy behind me, "Are you checking in, Sir?"

"Yeah," he answered, "But I think I've got good news for your buddy over here, because I have two rooms reserved and I only need one of them." So I ended up getting the second room that he had reserved.

By 10:30 I was checked in. I was glad to be in a hotel after all. The big blister on my heel came apart that night. Since it was open, I started cutting most of that skin off. Underneath it there was another blister almost as big. It, too, had torn. So I started cutting that one off as well. Pretty soon, I had two big flaps of skin coming off my heel. Under those was a third blister, about the size of a quarter which was also coming apart. I had three layers of blisters — sort of like those hollow, wooden, Russian dolls, one inside the other. When I looked at my left foot, the blisters on that one were coming apart, too. I spent some time cutting off dead skin before taking a shower and going to bed.

I took a lot of pictures of my feet during all this travail. They're pretty disgusting, however. I'm not going to share them.

I decided to give up on the idea of sleeping out and to stay in hotels, motels or whatever came my way all the way home. People were not offering to put me up. I guess I can understand that, too. Sometimes, I'm kind of naive.

July 25th
Oxford, Ohio to Richmond, Indiana

The next morning, Wednesday, I headed toward Richmond, Indiana, but without a whole lot of optimism. I felt like I was walking on hamburger. I decided to try to just walk to the other side of Oxford — to the last hotel in town or something.

Just before 11:00 I came to a coin-operated laundry. Since I didn't have any clean socks, I went in and washed my two dirty sets of stuff. They didn't dry very well, but at least they were clean.

By 12:20 my feet were hurting — again. I had walked past the last restaurant about a mile and a half or two before. I thought it was too early then. Now I wished I had stopped to get something to eat because I could see at least a mile down the road, and there didn't seem to be anything but open country, and of course, my feet hurt — already.

About 1:30 I ran out of steam. I stopped at a driveway on the right and asked the lady who lived there if I could sit under her tree. It felt so good to get off my feet for a while.

After 20 minutes or so, I asked how far it was to a restaurant or something. The lady said there was a restaurant a half a mile up on the right. The next place with a motel, however, was Liberty — about eight miles past the little restaurant. Eight more miles didn't sound like a possibility for me that day. I had already walked four or five miles and by now I was stopping often.

I started hobbling up to the restaurant. The son of the lady who owns the house I had been sitting in front of pulled up next to me about 1/10 of a mile down the road, and asked if I'd like a ride to the restaurant. I thanked him profusely and got in his truck. He drove me to College Corner which is right on the Ohio/Indiana border. The town is about four blocks long and two blocks wide.

He apologized for not being able to give me a ride up to Liberty, but he had to get to work. He drove me to Carl's restaurant. As he drove into the parking lot, a car drove out. He said, "I think that was Carl. I used to work for him." I got out of the truck and he headed back south toward Oxford.

Carl was, indeed, gone and his little restaurant was closed.

I leaned against the lamppost in the middle of the little parking lot at Carl's. I could see past the end of the little town and a long way down the road. Lots of corn. Nothing else. Can you spell discouraged?

My feet hurt so bad….

After a while, I stuck out my thumb. Lo and behold, the first vehicle pulled over and a general contractor offered me a ride into Liberty. It was such a blessing to sit down. As I was finding room for my backpack in the cramped foot well I heard him say he "felt compelled" to give me a ride. He didn't notice me staring at him, and kept on talking. He told me there was a little motel in Liberty, a quick mart (part of a gas station) and a local pizza place. There was nothing after Liberty for 14 miles or so to Richmond. Unemployment was pretty high, he said.

"But the corn is a good eight feet high," I said, looking out the window, "the farmers, at least, must be happy."

"Yeah," he said, "it looks good, but there's no ears."

"What?" I asked.

He said because of the drought there was enough moisture for the stalks to grow, but the plants wore themselves out before they could grow ears. "What corn there is," he said, "the kernels are so little it isn't good for much except silage." Farmers, he said, were losing a couple hundred dollars per acre. He said it was the same thing with soy. It looked good, but there wasn't anything there that was worth much.

He dropped me at the Liberty Motel and drove off. He had only driven me a couple of miles. I had been so interested in what he was saying about the lousy crops that I hadn't gotten his name.

I hobbled up to the motel. On the door was taped a hand-written sign that said, "No Vacancy." I tried to tell myself it was a mistake, and walked in anyway.

"Please tell me that sign is wrong," I said to the lady behind the desk.

"Nope," she said, "We're booked up."

"Ooooooh…" I said, "Where's the nearest motel going north?"

"Not 'til you get to Richmond," she answered.

"Now, how am I going to get 14 miles to Richmond?" I said, under my breath.

"If you go next door," she said, pointing out the window to a little strip mall, "to the first door there, that's the unemployment agency. They'll get you a ride to Richmond."

I thanked her and hobbled next door. I sat for an hour or so until someone was free to drive me to Richmond. Eventually, a fellow who worked there drove me to the Comfort Inn at the north side of town. They, thank God, had a room. I was worried about trying to put my boots back on after I took them off. So after I checked in, I left my backpack at the desk, and hobbled across the parking lot to the nearest restaurant — Bob Evans — where I had dinner.

When I got back and took off my boots, things didn't look so good. Part of the blister on my left foot was filled with blood and extremely painful.

I knew I wasn't going anywhere soon, but the Comfort Inn didn't have Internet access. So I called the other motels in town and found the Holiday Inn on the east side of town did. I made a reservation there through the weekend starting the next night.

I was so disheartened. I considered giving up. All the time in motels resting my feet didn't seem like what I was supposed to be doing. Although I had come more than halfway (about 320 miles), I had ridden about 120 miles or so.

On the other hand… that meant I had walked about 200 miles….

I called Sam Nesmith and told him how discouraged I was. A man of action, he asked me what I had done. He told me to put together a T-chart with advantages and disadvantages of continuing. "What have you learned while you were sitting?" he asked. "Are there books about the place you're in? Maybe something like that will open up a whole new world for you. Don't just sit there going around in circles," he said.

If you have to stop, you have to stop, was what he told me. But hadn't I done what I felt I was supposed to do? After all, what I felt I should do was to "Take a walk." No destination was implied. No time limit was set.

I felt good about the people I had met and the sights I had seen. How far I had come didn't seem so important.

The next morning, Thursday, July 26, I checked out of the Comfort Inn and had a cab take me to Reid Hospital — quite a nice hospital, for a town of 38,000. The doctor there was concerned that I might have an infection on the bone beneath that blood-filled blister on my left foot. She had three X-Rays taken. But everything was OK. She gave me a prescription for Bacitracin ointment and told me to use it twice a day for two or three days and stay off my feet. She sounded a little stern when she told me to get off my feet.

I took a cab to the Holiday Inn and checked in. I asked the desk clerk, Melissa Mayberry, where the nearest restaurant was. She told me if I turned right when I walked out of the hotel there was a Bob Evans "just a block away." Once again, I left my backpack at the desk and hobbled out the front door. When I got to the main road, Route 40, and looked to the right I could see the Bob Evans. But it was at least a quarter mile away. Across the road from the hotel, however, was a Red Lobster restaurant. It was so much closer. I hobbled across Route 40 and had dinner.

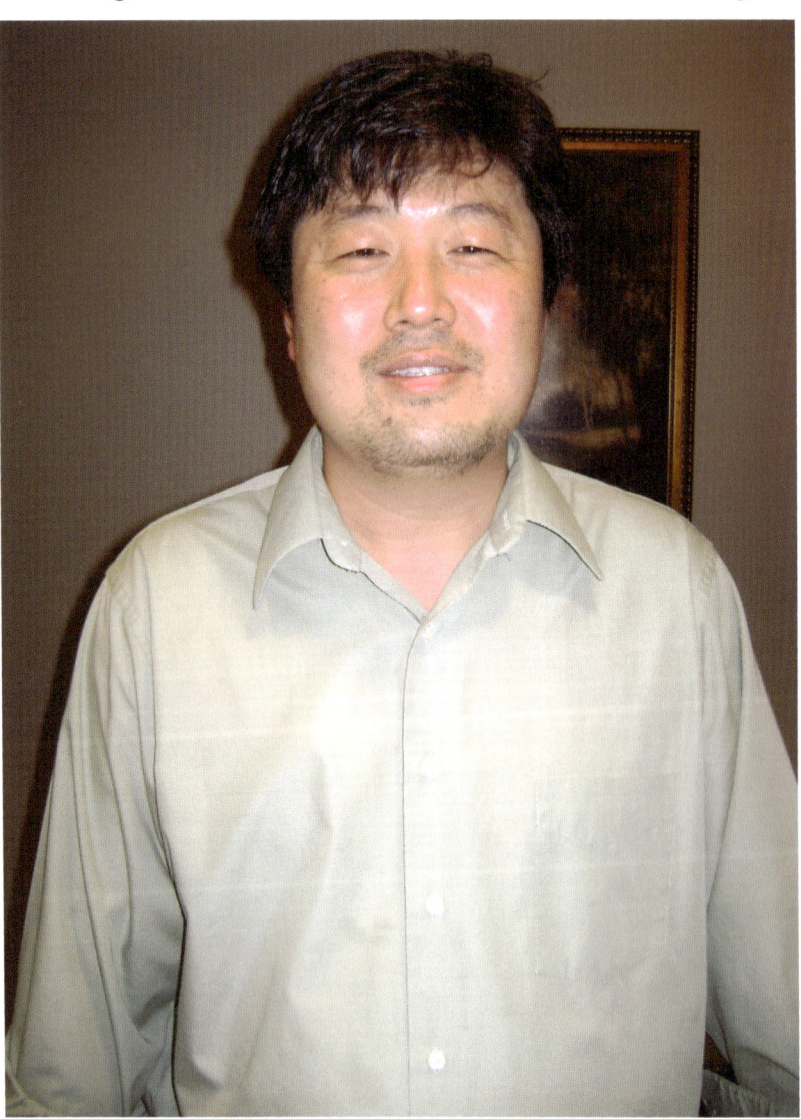

When I got back to the hotel and up to my room, I washed and dried what was left of my feet, anointed them with Bacitracin, and followed the doctor's orders.

Covering all my bets, I called home Friday and asked my daughter and my mom to send me my walking shoes and some socks. The boots are good boots, but I decided I needed to pamper my feet as much as possible.

Friday, Daniel Yoon, the manager at the Holiday Inn, introduced himself while I was working on the guest computer. I told him what I was doing, and he began to talk about his beliefs. He grew up in South Korea and went to church because if he didn't, he said, he'd get a spanking. When he was older, he had a brain tumor and was in horrible pain for a long time.

He said his Sunday School teacher's mother was a holy woman who lived on Prayer Mountain. She was so busy she could only come to her daughter's church (the one he went to) once in a while. One time she saw in the church bulletin that Daniel had a brain tumor. She said she knew when she read his name that she needed to talk with him. They talked for three hours. She said she never talked with any one person for more than 30 minutes. She just didn't have the time.

While they were talking, she put her hand on his chest. He said it felt like something had blown through him. He felt like something had entered him — filled him. He can't describe what it was, but he said from that time he felt at peace, in spite of the pain that had tormented him for so long. The brain tumor disappeared. Daniel went to seminary — first in South Korea and later in the U.S. — for a total of eight years or so. But he drifted out of the ministry and into what he's doing now.

When I told him how important I thought Jesus' command to "love one another" was, he spoke for a long time. His feeling is that the most important thing is to love God — that loving someone else is something we do for our own benefit. The act of loving someone, in and of itself, is meaningless unless we love God. When we love God, loving someone else is something we do for ourselves — because it makes us feel so good, so complete. Essentially, we agreed, you can't love your neighbor unless you love God — and *vice versa.*

He said the reason we want to go to Heaven is not for any of the *things* there, but because when we truly love someone, we want to be with that person. We long for that person, and don't feel whole until we are with them. When we are with them we feel such joy.

Daniel was so inspirational! It was such a joy to talk with him. I wish I had turned on the little recorder I was working with when he and I talked. I asked him the next day to read through what I had written. He said I had captured it well.

The shoes arrived Saturday morning. By then, my feet looked better and felt better, but it was still a little painful to walk on them — even with the shoes in place of boots.

I took a cab to the Central United Methodist Church Sunday. Pastor Scott Bell spoke about *Saints with Crooked Halos* — regular people like you and me who aren't perfect, but sometimes, somehow, manage to be the people we're supposed to be. I liked the message. I also liked the women's trio that sang.

That weekend there had been a Little League tournament for 11-year-olds. Starting Friday afternoon, several of the teams stayed at this Holiday Inn. There was precious little adult supervision. There must have been 50 or more 11-year-old boys along with their siblings running around like little maniacs — playing volleyball in the hotel lobby, running through the corridors screaming and giggling until at least midnight. If the parents were present, they hadn't even looked like they were concerned about this behavior.

Sunday I asked Melissa, "Is it just me, or are these kids incredibly obnoxious?"

"Oh. It's not you at all!" she replied. Melissa said they had to refund part of several customer's charges because of their complaints about noise.

My father and mother would have beaten me senseless if I had acted like those kids….

I decided that Monday, I would walk the six or eight miles back across town to the Comfort Inn. If my feet held up as well as I think they would, I would leave Tuesday and head toward Ft. Wayne.

The minuscule maps I had showed there are little towns every eight or 10 miles on the way — with the exception of a couple of long intervals. Hopefully, by then my feet would be up to 15 miles or more a day.

Once again I thought of the men who, during the Civil War, marched north and south from one end of our country to the other and back. Many of them had no shoes at all. Of all the diseases and other conditions that afflicted those people, sore feet rarely get even a fleeting mention in the histories of those days.

And here I was — a tenderfoot, indeed. Once again, I regretted the days I spent sitting barefoot in hotels.

On the other hand, Daniel Yoon was another fascinating person I would have missed if I hadn't had to stop to rest my feet....

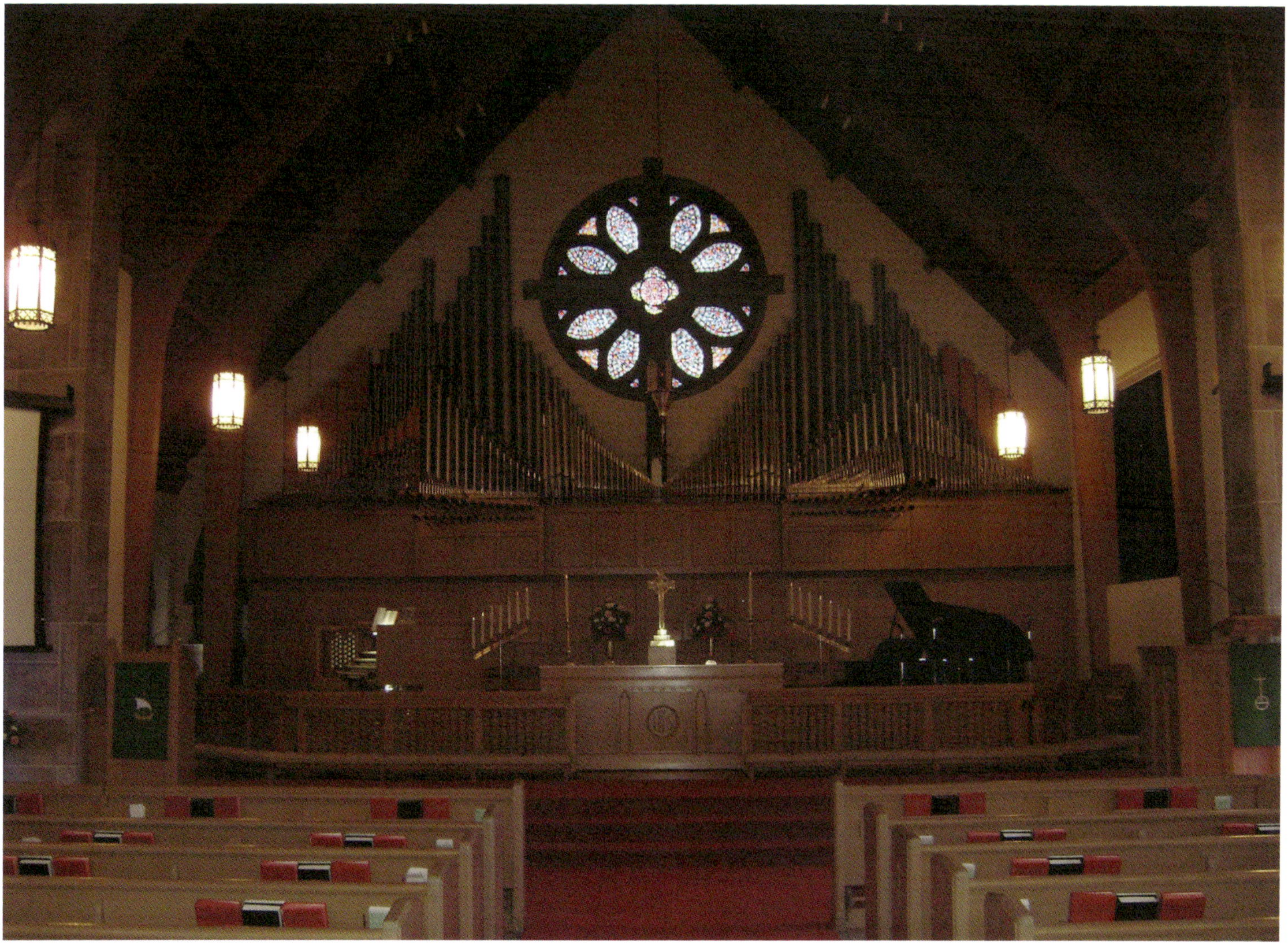

July 30th
Richmond to
Richmond, Indiana
(Huh?)

I left the Holiday Inn in Richmond about 9:00 on Monday, July 30, walking slowly to give my feet a rest. I stopped by a UPS store and mailed my boots back to Kalamazoo. The walking shoes felt easier on my feet. And here in Indiana I shouldn't see any rattlesnakes. There probably wouldn't be as much danger of twisting my ankle, either — lots of flat land in Indiana.

I stopped at the local WalMart, got some money out of the ATM, got a prescription refilled, bought some supplies including some walking socks, and headed out again.

I stopped at the Main Street Barber Shop. "Can you give a haircut to someone who's sweating like a pig?" I asked.

"Sure," she replied, "No problem."

So I got a haircut, which was kind of nice. I got my beard trimmed and my eyebrows trimmed while I was at it. I felt like a new man... I guess.

I walked to downtown Richmond. It's a pretty nice little town — a lot like Kalamazoo. It's got what they call Uptown — what I would call Downtown — where U.S. Route 40 and U.S. Route 27 cross (U.S. Route 40 going east and west and 27 going north and south). I had started at the Holiday Inn, way out east of town on U.S. Route 40 by the Interstate, and right near the Indiana/Ohio state line. Walking through Up(Down)town I was impressed by the shops and trees and benches. It's a very pleasant place to shop. And there weren't many boarded up storefronts, like there are in a lot of small towns.

I walked past the municipal building and stopped at a bench in front of the Manpower building to rest for a minute. Then I continued across the Main Street bridge. Pretty soon I saw a street sign that said West Third Street. "**West** Third?" I said to myself, "Wait a minute... I thought that Route 27 went north right in the middle of town. Shouldn't that be between East and West? Why am I at Third Street **West**?"

About three houses up there was a fellow standing on his porch. I walked up and asked him, "Where's Route 27?"

"Oh," he said, "You just walked past it. It's actually Ninth Street East."

"Oh, geez!" I said, "Twelve blocks?"

He said, "Yeah."

"Ahhh, Ahhh, Ahhh… OK…." I said, and turned around to walk back.

"Where are you going?" he asked.

I told him, and I said I was coming from Tennessee.

"Where in Tennessee?" he asked.

I said, "Sneedville."

"Whoa!" he exclaimed, "My wife's from Tazewell."

"Really?" I said, "Get out of here!" Tazewell is real close to Sneedville. Well, in Sneedville, real close is relative. Everything's about an hour drive from Sneedville.

We talked for a little bit, and I headed back east down Route 40. I went about a block and a little boy ran up behind me and he said, "Mister! Mister!"

"What?" I asked.

He held up a little sign and said, "Me and my buddy are selling Kool Aid. Would you like to buy a glass? It's 25 cents for a glass or 50 cents for a big glass."

"Well," I replied, "I don't really want any Kool Aid, but I'll buy a glass from you. I'll just give you the money and you can drink it yourself."

And he said, "Wow! Thanks!" Then he said, "50 cents? That's a real big glass!"

"Well, you and your buddy share it," I said, "But you **can** tell me where I should go for lunch."

His eyes got real wide. He pointed across the street and said, "Ooh! Pizza King!"

"Well, I don't think I want pizza," I said, "But thank you. I'll go up the street some."

So he headed back to his porch. It was about half a block to where Pizza King was and the closer I got the more I thought, "You know, I've seen four or five of these places. I wonder how the pizza is?" Like most people in my family, I'm a real pizza connoisseur (perhaps common-sewer is more correct).

So I went in. And the pizza is wonderful! And it's cheap! They have a special on Monday and Wednesday. You get an eight-inch pizza and all the Coke or iced tea or whatever you want to drink for $6.19! That's just ridiculous. It filled me up, and it was good — it was very good, actually.

I walked back across the Main Street Bridge and finally got to just before Ninth Street. I sat down on one of the nice benches they have under the trees downtown. Route 40 is cobblestone, and it's pretty. As I was sitting there, I noticed that across the sidewalk from me was a computer store. The sign on the door read, "Out to Lunch. Back at 2:00." It was 10 minutes 'til. At five minutes 'til the guy took the sign down, and I walked in. "Excuse me." I said, "I wonder if you could do me a favor?"

He said, "Sure."

I said, "Sure?"

He said, "Well… Maybe…."

"Smarter," I said, "I forgot to print this one piece of paper before I left the Holiday Inn this morning. And I need to know how far apart the towns are where I'm walking. I wonder if you could print it for me." So he did. He had to go through some typical computer shenanigans to find one that would accept my thumb drive and one that had a printer that would print what I wanted., and blah de dee blah de dee blah…. But he printed it for me, and he didn't charge me anything for it.

So now I knew how far I had to go every day to find a hotel.

Then I turned the corner and started walking up Route 27. I got about two blocks up and I said to myself, "You know… My feet are hot… And my right foot hurts… And I've come probably eight miles so far (especially if you add half a mile in each direction across the WalMart parking lot, and then the mile or so in each direction and the trip over to West Third Street and back in my big error). If I wreck my feet the first day out I'm going to feel stupid."

I was sitting in front of the Indiana Football Hall of Fame. So I walked up on the steps and called a cab. The guy was there in ten minutes, and he drove me over to the Comfort Inn. That's where I was Wednesday of last week. So I had a four-day time warp.

The Comfort Inn had a room, and it's cheap there. But, of course, they still didn't have a guest computer. They also don't have a coin-operated laundry nearby.

I looked at myself in the mirror, and discovered that the lady at the Main Street Barber Shop had skinned me! When she said, "How do you want your hair?" I said, "Well, make it about half as long as it is." So she did.

And then she said, "And, how do you want your beard?"

And I said, "Half, again." I meant half as long as it is now, and I think she thought I meant half again as short as what you just made my hair. So now my beard looks like a Don Johnson thing — half a day growth. So I look a little silly. But nobody I know is going to see me — at least nobody I know now. Of course, as Brother Dave said, "A stranger's nothin' but a friend you ain't met yet."

By 2:40 I had my feet up and my shoes off, and everything looked good. There wasn't any blood on my socks, which was a plus. And my feet felt pretty good.

Later, I went over to Bob Evans and had something to eat. I asked the lady at the desk at the Comfort Inn if it was possible for them to do a load of laundry for me. And she and the maintenance man said, "Noooo. They won't let us do that."

So I asked, "Where's the nearest coin-operated laundry?"

The maintenance man said, "Well, there's one just right down the street there."

"Where is that?" I asked.

He said, "Well, you go down here and you turn here and you go there…."

And I asked, "Well how long will it... how far is it?"

He said, "About six minutes."

"Well," I said, "I'm walking."

"Oh, no, no," he said, "It's not in walking distance. So forget about that."

I said, "Oh, crud!"

He said, "Why don't you put all that stuff in a bag, and I'll take it home and wash it for you and bring it back?" That's just what he did. His name is Dick Spires. I told him several times how much I appreciated it — especially since I had no clean clothes left. I offered him money, but he wouldn't take it.

July 31st
Richmond to Winchester, Indiana

At 8:45 Tuesday morning I left the Comfort Inn after doing the normal start-of-the-week stuff (clean out the water bladder in my backpack and fill it with ice and fresh water, put dirty clothes in a plastic bag, re-pack the backpack, etc.). It was a beautiful morning. About 70 degrees — maybe 75. Not a cloud in the sky. A little breeze. Not too humid. Of course by 1:00 the temperature got way up into the 80s and the humidity went up as well.

Just past the end of a construction zone was Chester Drive with a little subdivision. There were two marvelous little brick pillars about five feet tall that provided enough shade for me to sit in for a little bit.

Ten minutes later, a nurse who was on her way home from work turned around and came back to make sure I was alive — just to check and make sure I was OK. Wasn't that nice?

At the next place I stopped to rest, two people stopped and asked if I was alright or alive or whatever. A lady thought there might be a little restaurant in Fountain City, but no place to stay. Lynn was the next place and that's six miles past Fountain City. Fountain City, she said, is three or four miles up at least — maybe farther than that.

About 11:00, I stopped just before Wallace road, where the gentleman at the corner on the east side of the road has some lovely trees. I sat under them to rest. Across Wallace Road is Northeastern Junior/Senior High School, and the band and the color guard were already out practicing. It was beautiful sitting up there. There was a nice breeze. The weather was lovely — not too hot. It was absolutely beautiful! All you could see for miles in any direction was corn.

A couple months ago, this would have sounded boring, but I was beginning to really love it. When the traffic melts away — and it does, now and again — you can look across this beautiful country that God has given us. In many places, it looks much as it must have looked a couple hundred years ago. Often, I could hear cattle lowing from a long way away. I could feel the breeze in my face. Smell the corn — almost taste it. On many occasions, it touched me deeply.

Normally, we flash past these lovely scenes, intent only on the cars around us. That's a good thing — don't get me wrong. But not to take the time to be a part of the world around us... well, that's something we miss. At our peril, I think. If we continue to take it for granted, we may end up losing it altogether.

Up ahead, a road from the west intersected Route 27. I could see a young man walking toward Route 27. He appeared to be studying something he held in his hands. As I got closer, I could see he was wearing bib overalls, but I couldn't recognize what he was looking at so intently. Was it a book? When he turned north on Route 27 about 100 feet or so ahead of me, I finally realized he was watching a portable DVD player. He was so engrossed in whatever he was watching, I was concerned he might step off the shoulder into the roadway. Of course, nothing much was coming or going, so he wasn't in too much danger. It was funny to see him in the middle of all the beauty I had been so taken with, totally ignoring it. Familiarity breeds contempt, I guess. I never got close enough to see what he was watching.

At 11:25 there was a sign for the Family Diner.

About 1/10th of a mile after that there was a sign that showed a horse and buggy for the next mile. Maybe I would see some Amish folks.

Crossing the bridge, coming into Fountain City, I could see the Family Diner, about a block ahead. But that wasn't any half a mile! It was going to be 10 minutes 'til 12:00 by the time I got there. And 25 minutes meant I was walking at a mile-an-hour clip. I knew I was doing more than two. It seems even signs can't be relied on for accurate distance estimates.

108

I had dinner at the Family Diner. Today's Special, said the sign, was Beef and Noodles with two side dishes for $6.99. And it was good! And there was also a piece of apple pie that would knock your socks off.

There was only one problem — the waitress said there's no hotel, motel, bed and breakfast or anything else either in Fountain City or up the road about seven miles in Lynn. She said Winchester is the next place, and that's about 17 miles. Seventeen miles was not going to happen this day — at least not walking....

A sign said the Fountain City United Methodist Church was one block west. I thought perhaps there might be someone there who could give me some direction. It's a pretty white frame building with a bell in the belfry. No one was there, nor was there anyone in the education building next door. I went back to Route 27 and headed north again.

At 1:45 it was very quiet. I walked across the road to what looked like the last little teeny patch of shade heading north for a long while. I decided to rest there for a minute. I erased some files from my recorder so I could put more stuff on it.

I got a little tired of walking.... No, I got a lot tired of walking. And my left foot was starting to hurt. My right foot was starting to hurt... Well, they both were starting to hurt, but the left one in particular. I had only gone about half way to Lynn, and I was hurting pretty bad. I said to myself, "I'm not going to make it to Winchester today. That's not going to happen." That was truly a defeetist attitude.

But from what I was told, there was no place to stay in Lynn, and no place to eat, either. So, I gave a big sigh.... and stuck my thumb out. About 15 cars later I turned around to start walking again, and there was a lady backing up toward me. I hobbled toward here as fast as I could, hoping she wouldn't change her mind and pull away.

I looked in the window, and she said, "I'm going to Winchester. Do you want a lift?"

"That's exactly what I want." I said, "Thank you very much."

Her name is Rose Ballantine. When I told her tomorrow is my birthday, she said, "Oh! Today is my son's birthday!" She said he just turned 21. "I don't think I'm ever going to get him out of the house." She said he graduated from high school, but he hasn't found a job, and he hasn't looked real hard. She said he's not going to school, either.

He was working for a while, I guess, and then didn't make the 90 days that he needed to have some kind of job security. But she's taking him tomorrow to another place that does the same kind of work where he should be able to get in.

She's looking for a job at a chocolate company nearby. She's hopeful — a little. Jobs are hard to come by.

I told her she was crazy to pick up a big, sweaty guy. She told me she never picks up hitchhikers, but she "felt compelled" to give me a ride. While she chatted away, I sat in stunned silence — and it's not often that I'm unable to talk.

She drove me to the new hotel that had just opened in Winchester — the Randolph Inn and Suites. It was so new that they don't even have all the furniture in the rooms. The room had two beds, but it didn't have a chair in it yet. It's a very nice place.

When I was checking in I told Chris, the desk clerk, I was an old guy, AARP, ex military and all that sort of thing. "Well..." he said, "normally, the rate for these rooms is $80.95, but since we don't have all the furniture in, and we don't have all of this and all of that, the lowest I can give you the room for is $50.00 a night."

"Well, I'll take it," I said, "In fact, I'll take it for two nights, since tomorrow's my birthday."

I had thought if I walked all of it, that I would get to Winchester Wednesday night. It's not as though I was losing time — there's no deadline, after all. So I had gone from Richmond to Winchester. Having lived in Virginia for 30 years, it's hard for me to say Indiana and not Virginia after the names of these towns.

I took a much-needed shower. There are a couple of little local restaurants here. Rose said the Chicken Shack was a good place. And then Chris said that up on the other street that crosses Route 27, there's a local Mexican restaurant of some sort that's really good. I don't like Mexican food all that much, but I like to go to local restaurants whenever I can, so I figured I'd do that the next day.

My feet looked pretty good except the blood blister on my left foot was purple. That whole area in the front of my left foot was purple. The right foot was OK. Well... mostly OK.... A day and a half of resting was probably a good idea. And Thursday morning I would head out again!

I spoke with Clyde Shaffer who's one of the investors/owners of the Randolph Inn and Suites. He told me that this is predominately a Quaker town county, and is pretty conservative, and that he, in fact, goes to a Quaker church. He's a hog farmer who is now also part owner of a hotel. He told me the hotel just opened last Thursday.

I asked him how the Chicken Shack was. He said it's excellent. The folks who built the Randolph Inn & Suites are looking to put in a restaurant next door to the hotel, eventually, but they don't want the typical hamburger and French fries place. They want a place more upscale — where you can sit down and get a steak or something like that.

Clyde confirmed to me that Winchester is halfway between Dayton, Ohio and Muncie, Indiana. It's a big enough town that it has its own WalMart. I guess that's the clear indicator that where you live is no longer a small town.

When I was walking to the Chicken Shack for dinner I saw a sign that said it's 27 miles to Richmond, and 9 to Lynn. Of course, that would be downtown Richmond — a couple miles past the Comfort Inn. And I was mostly to Lynn when Rose picked me up. So I probably walked about 10 miles today. Rose gave me a ride the other 10 or so. The Chicken Shack did, indeed, have excellent chicken.

Wednesday afternoon I talked to Ken Cook, who was the general contractor for the hotel construction. He gave me a little information about hotels up the road so I could find a couple of places to stay. I called the Holiday Inn at the next town — no vacancies. So I called the Super 8. They are going to put me up Thursday night, if I can make it all the way there to Portland, Indiana — that's a 19-mile trip.

The next day to Berne is something like 16 miles. But the Black Bear Inn in Berne is the one the Randolph Inn and Suites folks used for a model. So I decided that was where I would try to spend Friday night.

I called the Black Bear Inn and made a reservation there. The rest of the day I sat on my butt in my room. I wanted to make sure my feet were well rested before the next hike. I talked with some people on the phone who called to tell me happy birthday, and that was about all I did. Good for the feet, I guess. And the phone calls were good for the soul....

All that sitting gave me ample opportunity for thought. I had always believed I would live to be 100. It's easy to forget that death can come at any time. But when a fellow stuck a gun in my face in a robbery in 1973, a lot of things that concern most people stopped being so important for me. The open-heart surgeries made me even more aware of my mortality. Tom Lehrer said, "It is a sobering thought that when Mozart was my age, he had been dead for two years." In my case, a lot longer than that. And what have I done that will be remembered after I'm gone?

I had hoped this journey would provide some answers — some guidance. Surely this wasn't about learning how to take care of my feet.

But an ethereal revelation just wasn't forthcoming.

Perhaps the journey *is* more important than the destination — the striving, the persistence, continuing to put one foot in front of the other on the right path. And, of course, being open and accepting and trusting.

But then, finding the *right* path. That, of course, is the trick.

August 2nd
Winchester to
Berne, Indiana

I left the Randolph Inn at 7:27 a.m. I wanted to get an early start, because this was to be a 20-mile day, and I didn't even know if I would be capable of a 20-mile day. But I had been told by about four people that there was nothing before Portland. So, one way or another, that's where I was determined to end up.

The temperature was supposed to be about 73 degrees. That seemed about right. The air felt kind of thick — muggy. I hoped that would go away. A little breeze would have been welcome, too.

Just before 8:00, having come a mile and a half or so, all the need, the drive, the urge, the feeling that I needed to continue to walk seemed to ebb away. I had the image of someone pulling the plug in a bathtub — the urge just ran out of me. I stopped walking, looked around, and said aloud, "Is that it? Am I done?"

Nearby, there was a left turn into a factory and a right passing lane for people going north. There was a tree there that looked like it was the last piece of shade for at least a mile. So I sat there for a minute, cooled down a little, had some water and thought about what I had just felt.

I could turn on my cell phone and call someone to come and get me. Ten or twenty people in Kalamazoo had offered to come to my aid if I needed it. Somehow, though, that didn't seem right — even though I had already convinced myself taking rides from strangers was OK.

So just what did that feeling mean? Once again, I was in a quandary. There didn't appear to be any logical solution. Then again, logic hadn't been much of a factor in any of the decisions about this journey.

As I sat there, I had the feeling that someone was going to pull over and ask how far I was going. When I said "Kalamazoo" he was going to say, "That's where I'm going." I decided if that happened, I would go with him. Otherwise, I would just continue to put one foot in front of another.

I didn't understand why I should be thinking about quitting just as my feet were mostly well, either. There was a lot I didn't understand....

It took longer to describe all this thought process than it did to go through it. By five after 8:00 I had started walking again.

At 8:30 I made a little movie looking up and down Route 27. Then I sat in somebody's front yard under their shady trees. A couple of those big stock trucks rolled by. I thought they must have been going back to Sneedville to join the one that never moves at Mulberry Gap. Hah!

Just before Rogersville, as I was walking along, a guy pulled up across the road, heading north, and said, "Do you want a lift?"

"Where are you going?" I asked.

"I'm going up here to Rogersville." he said, "Where are you going?"

"Kalamazoo," I replied.

"Michigan?" he asked.

I said, "Yeah."

"Well, I'm not going that far," he said, "But come on… I'll give you a ride."

So I got in the car. And we drove maybe a mile or two. He wanted to put in an employment application at a place, so he said, "If you don't mind, I'll go over and put this employment application in and drive you to Portland."

And I said, "Well… OK… I guess… That's fine."

His name is Brian Buck, but you call him Buck. He has three children — a 21-year-old son, a 19-year-old daughter, and a 17-year-old son who's in jail in LaPorte. Buck said prison, then corrected himself and said "in jail." I guess prison is harder time than jail.

While he was inside putting in his employment application I noticed a cup full of pennies in the car. When he got back in I asked him, "What's that?"

"If I need it," he said, "That's to buy enough gas to get home."

"I'll buy you some gas," I offered.

"No. No," he said, "I'll be alright."

"No," I said, "I'm buying your gas. I don't want to hear any argument."

After we got some gas, he said, "I'll give you a ride up to Portland. I think I've got enough gas to get up there and back now."

So he drove me to Portland. Before we got to the Super 8 motel where I had a reservation he said, "Before we get to the Super 8, I want to go to this place over here across the way." He wanted to talk to his girlfriend who works for a company there that makes fans. When he got back in the car he said, "You know, I don't have anything to do. Where are you going after Portland?"

"Well," I said, "I'm supposed to go to the Black Bear Inn in Berne."

"Well," he said, "I'll just give you a ride up there."

"No. No. No," I protested, "You've already given me a ride…"

"No. I've got nothing to do," he said, "and you just bought me gas. Come on. I'll drive you up to the Black Bear Inn."

When I told him I was going to Kalamazoo after we'd been riding for a while, Buck said, "Gee! If I didn't have something to do this afternoon, I'd just drive you up there. Wouldn't that be nice? Just drive and talk and have a good time...."

I almost said, "Why don't you just drive me up there?" Hah. Hah. "I'm ready."

So I ended up in Berne that day at the Black Bear Inn, less than 30 miles from Fort Wayne. He drove me about 17 miles. Maybe more. And it's a good thing he did. There were no hotels, no motels, no restaurants — not much at all — between where he picked me up in Portland until we got to Berne.

I spoke with Jerre Nichols who works at the hotel. I told him Ken Cook at the Randolph Inn and Suites said they had used the Black Bear Inn as a model for their hotel. He wanted to know how it had turned out. We talked about my journey for a long time.

Later, in my room, I thought when I left Berne, there probably won't be places to eat or sleep for the 14 miles until I got to Decatur. I saw long days of cornfields in my future....

Anyhow, I was in Berne. I planned to walk over and have some lunch after I called the Super 8 motel Buck had driven me past in Portland and cancelled my reservation there. And then I had to figure out how to get through more hours of sitting on my butt. This trip was turning into an exploration of hotels and motels. And, once again, I was discouraged by it. Was I doing the right things? Around and around. One more time.

My feet felt pretty good, but I kind of felt like I had walked enough....

I thought....

Whatever....

August 3rd
Berne to Decatur, Indiana

On Friday, I left the Black Bear Inn just before 9:00 and headed north. The sign said Decatur 12, Ft. Wayne 34. And the shoulder narrowed for a while, so if I jumped off, I'd be in the corn.

After a while, the shoulders got pretty wide again, but I had to dodge a lot of horse apples from the Amish buggies. I figured that was better than rattlesnakes....

Five or six miles out of Berne, Jerre, from the Black Bear Inn, pulled over across the road and said, "Hey. I'm going about a mile or two up the road. Do you want a ride?"

And I said, "Well... Yeah... OK."

The sign at the intersection where Jerre dropped me off said Decatur 6. At that intersection Route 27 turns into a four-lane, divided highway.

A little after 10:00 I needed a rest. So I sat down next to somebody's driveway. It looked like the last piece of shade for at least a mile on the east side of the road. There hadn't been enough shade on the west side of the road to qualify. So, I stretched out, and had a little water, and wanted some more.

I had seen a sign about half a mile before that said "McDonald's 5 miles in Decatur," and about a half mile before that there was one that said, "Long John Silver's 6 miles." I figured if there were two fast food restaurants within half a mile, hopefully there would be a motel nearby.

A little later I made a little movie of the longest straight stretch of road I had seen since I started this trip. When you look at that little movie you can see there's hardly any shade anywhere very near the road. You can see three or four miles north and three or four miles south. For that matter, you can see three or four miles east and three or four miles west. Lots of soy beans and lots of corn. Not much of anything else.

The countryside had changed dramatically since I set out more than a month ago. The lush green hills and valleys of Tennessee and Kentucky had given way to amber waves of grain stretching as far as you could see in all directions. What a beautiful country we live in!

Ahead, I could see a road coming from the east. There was a house set back from the intersection with Route 27, and from behind that house came a pony pulling a little buggy carrying two Amish girls. The driver might have been 10 years old and the other girl was about five or six — pretty close to the ages of my granddaughters. They turned south toward me. I crossed Route 27 so I was on the east side of the road. When they went by they waved at me from across the road. They looked so sweet in their bonnets and dresses. I really wanted to take a picture of them for Lily and Viola, but I didn't, for fear of embarrassing them. Viola, my youngest granddaughter, absolutely loves horses, and would have been so envious of them.

At about five minutes after 11:00 I figured I must be almost to Decatur. I looked up the road and could see at least one sign up on a tall pole. I had been walking pretty steadily, except a 15-minute break and a one- or two-minute ride since five minutes 'til 9:00. That's two hours. And I'd been walking pretty fast. I'd say I'd made about six miles. Hopefully, more than that.

At 11:42 a sign said, "Decatur, Welcome." The next sign said, "Days Inn. 2 miles ahead on left. $35.00 and up." About a half mile past the "Welcome to Decatur" sign there was a WalMart on the left side of the street. I went in there to get some Mole Skin and some new socks. I didn't like the ankle socks I had bought in Richmond. Once again, it seemed like a good half mile from Route 27 to the door of WalMart. I was getting sensitive to those little extra walks. I had lunch at the Subway in Walmart — glad to take advantage of the air conditioning.

About 1:30 before I got to the Days Inn I had seen advertised on the sign, there was a Comfort Inn. I got lucky and got the last no smoking room there. They not only had a guest computer — the first question I asked — but they also had a guest laundry. So, when I finished taking a shower I took all my dirty clothes downstairs and threw them in the wash.

As I was going to the WalMart I saw this strange little sign. It was on the side of a building with a sidewalk (and curb) in front of it. I studied it for a long time before deciding that some things just are not meant to be understood.

I talked to Jami Murray[13] while standing in line in the WalMart. She was getting things in preparation for a 500-mile bicycle trek through West Virginia that she and her husband were going to participate in with their church. That sounded like a very ambitious project! I worried about them on two-land highways in the mountains and kept them in my prayers.

August 4th
Decatur to
Fort Wayne, Indiana

Saturday morning, I went down to the hotel lobby for the complimentary breakfast. The room was full, so I took my cereal and juice out onto the patio behind the building. While I was eating, two women asked if they could share my table. They were Pam Vaughn and Paula Woodruff, members of a church group heading to a prayer retreat. Pam thought her husband, Dave, who is the pastor at their church, would like to know about my journey. They prayed for me, then we talked until it was time for them to leave.

At 8:40 I left, too. I made it to the north end of town by 9:30. I went to the Decatur Gardens, the last restaurant — the last anything, it turned out — heading north. I had a little breakfast, figuring I won't see anything to eat for a couple hours at least. Maybe a lot longer

than that. I walked over to the Hallmark store in the little shopping center right next door, bought some stamps, and mailed the little tiny socks I don't like home. By 10:15, I was on the road again.

Just north of Decatur is the Saint Mary's River. I had been looking at rivers and creeks as I walked along. This was a pretty little river and it was flowing well, despite the drought. But, just like all the others that I've seen, it was full of junk. I counted five regular tires, a tractor tire, and a couple of 10-gallon buckets in various stages of decay, as well as other assorted crud lying in this pretty little river. It would be nice if we actually valued this beautiful country we live in. But apparently, some of us don't....

It was a beautiful day, though. About 9:00 while walking through Decatur I saw a bank sign that said it was 68 degrees. It wasn't nearly as humid as it was the day before and there was a little breeze. Up ahead were some cirrus clouds, but it was pretty clear behind me. If it weren't for the noise of the cars on this grooved concrete highway, it would have been pretty much perfect.

At 10:45 I found a little diary on the west shoulder of Route 27 heading north. It had about 10 or 20 pages filled in. I didn't know what to do with it. About a quarter of a mile ahead there was a church whose sign read, "Lighthouse Assembly of God. I didn't know He had been disassembled.

There was a car parked in front of the church. So I walked across the road to the east side. I knocked on the door of the church, and a young man who was working in the church answered the door. He said he was a member there, so I asked him if the names in the diary rang a bell. He said no, but he'd give it to the pastor and see if somebody knew whose it was. I sat in the shade under the front of the church for about 10 minutes. Any excuse to take a break....

South of the church is a set of Coffindaffer Crosses[14] on the side lawn. I had never been close enough to a set of them to see that they actually have spikes on the middle cross.

At 11:10 I headed out. A few minutes later, I went by a sign that said North 27/North 23. Route 23 was the one I needed to take me up to Route 13 in Indiana which turns into Route 131 in Michigan and runs right by Kalamazoo.

Shortly after that, I saw what looked like an ambulance go by, but on the side and on the back window, instead of a red cross, there were red crescents. What was that all about? I wondered if there is a large Muslim community nearby.

About 11:30 I saw the first jet I had seen in weeks. It was basically above Route 27, heading kind of east, maybe a little south, at about 5,000 feet. Twin-engine, swept wing, probably going to Dayton. It was sort of strange. Even around Cincinnati I hadn't seen any jets — any airplanes at all, for that matter. Maybe I had just stopped looking....

At 11:40, I sat down in front of the house at 9680 on Route 27, in the last little bit of shade for quite some time. The folks there had a beagle that barked continuously. About three quarters of a mile or so up the road was something that looked like a gas station or quick mart. I thought I'd walk up there, and see if they had a place to sit down out of the sun.

From where I sat, way back down the road with a little curve factored in, it looked like a little mini mart with a red sign. But when I got up to it, it turned out to be a barn with a "Do Not Enter" sign for the crossover on the road. So I was still looking for a place to sit down out of the sun. It was noon.

At 10 after, I was pooped. I stopped by a pretty little white house by the road. It has a tree in the front by the east side. I was kind of running out of get up and go, and it looked like another mile to down over the next little ridge. Once again, it didn't look like there was any shade past that for a while.

At 12:20, I wasn't really rested, but there was a cloud of gnats there, and they were driving me crazy. It wasn't too hot yet, but the humidity was up. There was a little breeze now and again that I hoped would continue.

About 1:00, I came to the Saint John Lutheran Church, Missouri Synod, and I was pooped again. It's a beautiful building, out in the middle of the farmlands. It may be considered to be in suburban Ft. Wayne, but it's a long way away from town.

I sat under a tree there for a while. I figured I must have another four miles to go before I got to Hessen Cassel. MapQuest indicated that was a little place on the south side of Fort Wayne, where I-469 crossed Route 27. I had hoped it was large enough to have a motel, or at least a restaurant.

I hadn't been sitting very long when a sheriff came by. He stopped and wanted to know if I was alive or alright and what I was doing. After I told him, I asked him how far it was to the next hotel, and he said, "Ooh… I don't think there's any on this side of Fort Wayne. You're going to have to wait until you get across town. I'd say you're talking 10 or 15 miles just to get to Fort Wayne, then another four or five to get to the north side of town."

Ughhhhh… Map Quest didn't do very well there. Now, I didn't know what to do. I was pretty certain I wasn't going to make another 15 miles today. It was 1:15. I had been walking four and a half hours, and I spent about an hour of that sitting down. Three and a half hours walking, that was nine, 10 miles. No… Another 10 or 15 miles just wasn't going to happen.

About a half mile past Saint John's Church, I was walking on the east side of the road, trying to decide whether to hitch hike or not, and a car pulled over. Charlene Johnson[15] offered to give me a ride. She was driving an old Chrysler Corporation car with the muffler just about shot, and it was really noisy. I only understood about half of what she said — if that. I did understand her when she said, "I'm going to Fort Wayne, and I'll give you a ride...."

So, we drove and drove, and sure enough, the sheriff was right — it was probably 10 or 12 miles to where there were any hotels at all. All the way through town... on the other side of town... fairly near where Charlene lives, there's a Red Roof Inn. That's where I ended up.

I decided to stay that night and the next. I would go to church Sunday, the next day. And then Monday morning I would push off heading north up Route 33. I was right on Route 33, and it goes up toward Ligonier. Somewhere up there I would get to Route 13 which turns into Route 131 in Michigan and goes right to Kalamazoo.

I had about 100 miles to go still. And she saved me about 10, I would expect. It was a good thing, because there really wasn't much of anything south of town. There were one or two fast food restaurants once you got into town, but that was a good six or seven miles past where she picked me up.

Charlene said she had been having some hard times. She had a little baby in the back seat, and he was the cutest thing you've ever seen. He was giggling and playing, and I was reaching behind the front seat tickling his feet.

Charlene had said she had seen me when I was on the west side of the road. She was driving south when she went by me, and then when she got done with whatever she had to do down in Decatur and came back up, there I was walking on the east side of the road past the church, and she picked me up.

"Well..." I said, "You're a crazy lady to pick people up."

"Yeah..." she replied, "But if I feel like I should pick them up, I just pick them up. And that's OK. I'm not worried about that kind of stuff."

I told her there ought to be more people like her. She was a godsend to me, I'll tell you....

I checked in to the Red Roof Inn and took a shower. Then I went across the street to the Liberty Diner, a nice little family restaurant. It was very good. The owner grew up in Greece. He came to the U.S. years ago during political problems in Greece, and is now a very patriotic American. He runs a great restaurant. There were a few Mediterranean dishes and a lot of other things. Everything I had over the weekend was really good.

When I got back to the motel, I asked the desk clerk if she had a list of nearby churches. "Why, Fort Wayne is called the city of churches," she said, "There are a couple hundred churches here." She found a directory that listed all the churches cross-referenced by location and denomination. Despite the Red Crescent ambulance that had passed me on the highway, I didn't see any Muslim congregations listed.

There was only one Methodist church listed in northwest Fort Wayne, where the Red Roof Inn is. The motel had a little map that showed the street it was on, but it wasn't possible to tell exactly where the church was. I called the church, but no one was in the office. It was Saturday, after all. I figured I would take a cab out there, and then walk back, if it wasn't too far.

Sunday morning, August 12, I called Deluxe Taxi for a cab at 9:00. Perry Hiner picked me up about 9:20. It's a good thing I called early. The church was so far north of town I wished I had taken my backpack so I could just start walking after the service. I felt like I was halfway to Michigan! His cab fare was $18.00 — a far cry from the $6.00 fares in Richmond.

When I told Perry what I was doing, he said he had had several "snapshot visions" as he called them. Many times in his life, he had clearly felt like God was warning him about someone or telling him that someone was going to be influential in his life. We talked all the long way out to the church.

Covenant United Methodist Church is a beautiful building with lots of parking. They had three services that day — conventional services at 8:30 and 11:00 and a contemporary service at 10:00. I arrived about 9:40. There were a lot of people having coffee and mingling around — some who had attended the early service and some who were waiting for the 10:00 service.

I wandered around taking pictures of the building, inside and out. Decorative banners were everywhere. They were made by skilled parishioners. The wall behind the altar was made of brick, but designs had been carved into the bricks. I had never seen that before and was very impressed.

The band was warming up and they were enthusiastic, but they were way too loud for me. The parishioners seemed to like it. I guess between the tinnitus and the middle high frequency hearing loss, my ears just can't put up with that any more. I decided to just wait for the 11:00 service.

I wandered into the chapel. There was a woman there. When I asked if I was interrupting her, she replied that the church likes to have someone in the chapel on Sunday mornings in case someone needs another person to pray with or answer questions. She introduced herself as Faun Brown.

I asked if she was one of the people doing the Healing Partners ministry. I had picked up and read a brochure about that. At Covenant, people who have problems — physical, psychological, emotional or anything else, I guess — can call Faun or her partner and schedule a time to meet, either at church or at home. Faun's partner is a licensed massage therapist. During the session they talk about the person's problem or concern. The massage therapist tells the person what she and Faun will do. Then the person lies down on a massage table and the therapist and Faun put their hands on the person. After a time of silence, the therapist may, or may not (as agreed beforehand), massage the person. Faun prays aloud.

This ministry goes back to early Christianity — and of course, earlier than that. I know it was fairly common in churches and gatherings some time ago, but aside from *healers* who travel from place to place, I'm not familiar with it happening a lot today.

I asked her how the ministry was received. She said that she and her friend hadn't been doing it for very long, but that the response was very favorable. She said that she was glad the response was so good because it made her feel wonderful!

We talked for 30 or 40 minutes. She asked if she could pray for me, and I accepted her offer. She put her right hand on my left arm, and we bowed our heads. After a while, she put her left hand on my left forearm. Then she prayed about me. It was, in fact, wonderful!

Afterward, I complimented her on her ability to pray like that. That's something I have never been able to do. I guess when I was young I took Matthew 6:6 too much to heart:

But thou, when thou prayest, enter into thy closet, and when thou hast shut thy door, pray to thy Father which is in secret; and thy Father which seeth in secret shall reward thee openly.

I was so glad I had decided to skip the contemporary service.

I enjoyed the pastor's message at the 11:00 service, but the sound system left me cold. What is it with church sound systems? We have had problems with the one at my church in Kalamazoo, and several of the churches I attended on this trip had problems with theirs as well.

At Covenant in Fort Wayne, the sound system has numerous speakers set above the chancel area. I could hear Rev. Jan Funk's message well, but it seemed to be coming out of thin air, or perhaps it seemed to originate in my head. It was disconcerting to watch her, but feel like she was lip-synching. I guess that's better than not being able to understand what someone is saying. Maybe it's just another indication that my hearing is shot....

After the service, I talked with Rev. Funk a bit. Faun Brown must have gone home after we talked during the second service. I looked for her, but couldn't find her.

I went outside and stood around in the parking lot trying to decide whether to call a cab or walk back to the hotel. It was five or six miles back, I figured — more than an hour. It had rained before I left the hotel, but wasn't raining at the time. I decided to take a walk. That, after all, is what I had been doing for weeks.

The road had two lanes in each direction and no shoulders. The grass was still wet from the morning rain, so I tried to stay on the very edge of the roadway, facing traffic. Whenever cars were approaching in both lanes, I got onto the grass or whatever was next to the road. After close to two miles of this, I came to a gas station / quick mart and went in for lunch. The people who made the pizza I had for lunch must have put a lot of work into it. I have always maintained you have to work hard to make a bad pizza, and this one was a **bad** pizza.

As I walked, I kept thinking about the Healing Partners ministry and how wonderful I had felt when Faun prayed for me. John Wesley's feeling of being "strangely warmed" described it very well. I wondered how much stronger the impact would have been if a massage therapist had been working on me at the same time.

I have a friend back in Virginia who had cerebral palsy all his life. I have known Jay since the early 80's. In 2000, a friend of his convinced him to see a traveling faith healer from Australia. Just by touching Jay, he healed him. Now, I had been extremely skeptical about such claims before I saw Jay walk into a room after that experience. I've found room for belief, courtesy of Jay's experience.

I found myself not concentrating on my own safety as much as I should, and decided I didn't want to continue jumping into the wet grass at the last minute while cars whizzed past. With my waterproof boots, the water wouldn't have been a problem, but the walking shoes were getting wet, and I had a long way to go the next day. And I worried that I wouldn't be quick enough one time if my attention kept wandering. So I called Deluxe Taxi and eventually a cab came and took me back to the motel.

Including tips for the drivers and a little something for the collection plate, that church service cost me quite a lot. Faun Brown, however, made it well worthwhile.

August 6th
Fort Wayne to
Goshen, Indiana

Monday, I left the Red Roof Inn just before 9:00 and headed up Route 33 toward Ligonier, Indiana. I had walked nine or ten miles when Doug Pressler pulled up and offered me a ride. He was heading up to Churubusco, a couple miles up the road, so I rode with him.

Doug was interested in the walk and in the Sneedville mission. In fact, he thought it would be "awesome" to go to Sneedville next year to work with the kids. Doug is a drummer, and is a very intense young man. That was surprising — most of the drummers I've known are pretty laid back.

Doug didn't want to stop talking and he was running a little early, so he took me past Churubusco to the first place going north where you could get something to eat. We got to the Citgo station at the intersection of Route 9 and Route 33 in Merriam, Indiana about 12:45 and had lunch together. I had a bratwurst and a Coke, and he had a corn dog and a Fresca or something. I enjoyed talking with him.

He said after he went back to his ex wife's home in Churubusco to pick up his two-year-old daughter he would come back and pick me up. I figured a number of things might come up, so I wasn't counting on that. After Doug left, I finished my Coke and at about 1:10, I headed north again. Something did, indeed, come up. Though I heard from Doug later, I didn't see him again that day.

I found what appeared to be the last shade for the next mile or two heading north. I sat down under a tree in someone's front yard to take a break. After five or 10 minutes Louise Stang and her 11-year-old daughter came out to stand up the signs that had fallen next to where I was sitting in front of their house, and we talked for about 15 minutes. She thought there might be something in Ligonier, and maybe not. And she thought it was about 12 more miles. I left there about 2:45.

A few minutes later I went by this sign. I thought that was funny. Why would anyone bury a tavern there?

JOEL BRISTOL FIRST WHITE
SETTLER IN NOBLE COUNTY 4-4-1827
OWNED THIS LAND AND A TAVERN
BURIED ON THIS FARM

About 10 minutes 'til 4:00 I made it to the Wolf Lake Marathon. I went to the bathroom and when I came out, there was Louise. She said, "If I had known I needed gas for my mower, I would have offered you a ride up here." I had forgotten to take pictures of her and her daughter, so I took one there.

One of the workers there told me it's about 12 more miles to Ligonier. And 12 more didn't seem within the realm of possibility today. After I had a Coke, I left the Citgo station at a quarter after 4:00. I decided to try hitching a ride.

After a while, I looked south and didn't see anyone coming. I turned around and looked north. Nothing there either. I was in sort of a fugue state — not quite able to make myself start walking, not able to decide to do something else — sort of like an electric toy that has lost the next instruction in its little memory, jerking back and forth and doing nothing.

A Jeep pulled over and the driver asked if I wanted a ride. "Yes, thanks," I answered. Her name is Rachael Harbes and she said she was going to the Ace Hardware store in Ligonier to get a part for her mother's sink. "My brother manages the Ace Hardware store in Stevensville, Michigan!" I said, "What a small world."

She didn't think there were any hotels in Ligonier. Maybe in Goshen, about 20 miles past Ligonier. Twenty *more* miles? Ugh....

She said she grew up nearby, but didn't live there any more. She had just come to her mother's house to help out a bit and do some thinking about what she wanted to do next with her life. When I asked where she lived, she said, "D.C. Well, actually, Arlington. It's across the river...."

"I know where Arlington is," I interrupted, "I lived in northern Virginia for 30 years. In fact, my son just moved from Arlington to San Francisco."

As we were getting out of her car at the Ace Hardware store I offered to put her on the mailing list for the walk if she would write down her name and EMail address. "Why don't I just give you my card?" she said, handing me one.

"S.A.I.C.?" I said, "You work at S.A.I.C.? I worked there until 2002!"

"No!" she exclaimed, "Really?"

"I worked at the Skyline offices…" I started.

"I **live** at Skyline!" she said, "My office is just near there."

We stood in the parking lot and talked, and she said she really didn't have anything else to do except fix her mother's sink. She offered to drive me to Goshen, where there were hotels. I accepted. We talked all the way up there. Her business card says she's a "Geospatial Specialist." Her company, Object Sciences, was recently acquired by S.A.I.C., and she's not sure she's too happy being in an organization as big as that. I told her she ought to apply for the job that my son, Josh, is leaving. Sales, however, didn't interest her either.

Rachael took me to the Holiday Inn Express in Goshen which had a room. I was pretty exhausted. I figure I must have walked at least 17 miles and come a total of about 54 miles. That other 37 miles was pretty empty. The endless vistas of corn were still beautiful, but they didn't offer any shelter from the sun. And hotels and restaurants were few and far between. I was so thankful for the rides I had that day — especially for Rachael "going the extra mile" (OK, the extra 20 miles or so) to take me on to Goshen!

August 7th
Goshen, Indiana to
White Pigeon, Michigan

I left the Holiday Inn Express in Goshen at five after 9:00. Goshen is a couple miles west of the road I wanted to be on. When I asked the hotel manager how to get to Route 13 north, he said to head down Route 33 south a mile or so, then take County Road 38 east to 13. Indiana Route 13 turns into Route 131 when you get up into Michigan. I wasn't too happy about walking south, but on the other hand, Rachel had saved me a whole lot of walking north the day before.

I'd walked nearly a mile when Rick Wright pulled up across the street heading south. He said, "Do you want a ride?"

Rick sells packaging and had just stopped to buy a cup of coffee. His van was full of samples and stock, but he made room for me. I told him where I was headed. He had planned to catch Route 13 farther south than where it intersects Route 38, but he decided to go the way I was going so I wouldn't have to backtrack. I'm really glad he did because Route 38 is a lousy walking road — no shoulders and embankments on both sides leaving no place to jump off should someone come too close. He dropped me off at Route 13 and headed south.

By 9:25, I was headed north. A couple dogs were barking at me from a farm across the road. For a minute I was afraid they'd come across the road after me and I'd have to use pepper spray on them. But they didn't.

About 10 after 10:00, I came to the road to Honeyville and took a picture of the sign. What a name for a town! Shortly after that, Route 13 was blocked, except to local traffic. A detour sign pointed east. I watched a couple of cars drive what looked like a half mile that direction before making a left and heading north again. I decided to consider myself local and kept going up the road. No one was working then, but the construction was just to rebuild a little culvert bridge about a tenth of a mile north. Fortunately, they had already put in the new bridge and were just working on the approaches and landscaping. I just walked across the new bridge. It wasn't finished for cars yet, but it was walkable. It would have been quite an additional walk if I'd followed the detour.

I hadn't gone a tenth of a mile past the construction area when a dump truck pulled up next to me. The driver said he had a load to deliver to the bridge site, but he couldn't see anyone there. Had I seen anyone? I told him no one was there, and offered to let him use my cell phone to call his office. He had his own cell phone, he said, and then asked where I was going. He was impressed. He asked if I wanted a ride, assuming no one was at the site. I thanked him, but said I was feeling pretty good and would just walk on. He drove down to a driveway near the little bridge, used his cell phone, and then drove back north. We waved as he went by.

As I was leaving the construction area, a block or two ahead a driver was trying to get his 18-wheeler turned around using a farmer's driveway. The farmer didn't look too happy about having tire tracks across part of his lawn. The driver waved at him, and got out to talk. The farmer lost his sullen look and, pointing this way and that, seemed to be giving the truck driver directions on how to get around the road work. The 18-wheeler drove off and the farmer went back to mowing his lawn. When I walked past I waved and smiled at the farmer. He waved back and sort of shrugged his shoulders.

About a tenth of a mile farther along a fellow heading south in a station wagon pulled up next to me. Donald Carson works for a delivery company based in Kalamazoo. He asked me how I had come through the construction site and how he might get around it. I told him he must have missed the detour sign. I pointed out the road off to the east that he should have been on. I told him the farmer seemed to give the driver of the 18-wheeler different directions. Donald drove down, talked to the farmer and came back by me. He said the farmer had, indeed, told him another way to get where he was going. He wished me luck.

When I went past the detour point, I could see how all the drivers had missed the detour sign. That poor farmer must have had a busy day.

I took a little break at the point where the detour began. As I rested, I wondered. If he offered, would I have taken a ride back to Kalamazoo from Donald? It had been four days since the will drained out of me. I had been walking on autopilot since then.

I stood up, strapped on my backpack, and put myself on autopilot again....

At five after 11:00 I took another break under a tree right where Route 4 crosses Route 13.

At five minutes 'til 2:00 I got to the Quick Mart in Middlebury, Indiana. I sat down and had a Blimpie sandwich, which was pretty lousy, and three Cokes. Whoo! I was just a little dry! I asked a woman where the nearest hotel/motel/bed & breakfast/whatever was going north. She said, "Oh, there's a charming little inn. It's about a half a mile on the left."

Well... As you can imagine, I left at 10 minutes after 2:00 and I got to the Country Victorian Bed & Breakfast at about a quarter of 3:00. That sounds more like more than a mile — close to two or three. Once again, distances are deceiving, I guess.

Nobody was there. So I called the number on the door and the lady said, "Oh, we're shopping. We'll be back around 4:00."

"Well," I said, "I'll just sit here on your porch."

But then I decided to walk right across the street under a shady tree in front of the elementary school and stick my thumb out for an hour and see if somebody would give me a ride home.

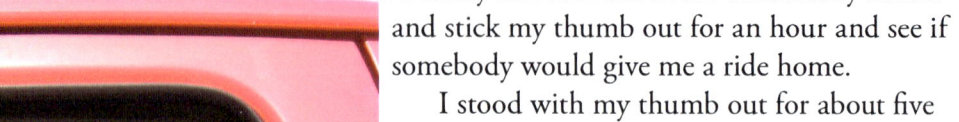

I stood with my thumb out for about five minutes and nothing happened. About half a block north was a homemade ice cream place, and that sounded pretty good to me. I thought I would get some homemade ice cream. Then I'd sit for a while before going back to the bed & breakfast."

I started walking up the street, and just as I got to the place and was about to walk across the parking lot, a guy pulled up next to me and asked, "Do you need a ride?"

I chuckled and said, "Yeah... OK... Sure... Where are you going?"

He said, "I'm going to White Pigeon."

"Yeah... That'll work," I said, "Let's go to White Pigeon."

His name is Rick Noble, he works at Jayco, a company that makes travel trailers in Middlebury. He said he had been in a class the year before with a guy who runs a motel in White Pigeon. "You'll like him," Rick said, "He's an ex-Marine."

He stopped just before we got to the Michigan border and went into a convenience store to get some stuff. I sat in the truck. Then we drove to White Pigeon.

Michigan! I was nearly home!

He took me to the Little Country Inn on U.S. 12, just east of Route 131. It's a 50's era motel — what used to be called a motor lodge. Larry and Caroline Hayes run it. Larry wasn't there when I arrived. Caroline said they had a room, but they don't have any non-smoking rooms. I couldn't be picky, so that's where I stayed.

As it turned out, the smoke smell wasn't too bad. The room had a little air conditioner, a little television, a little microwave, and a little refrigerator and a big bed. It was $29.95, and you can hardly beat that. I took a shower and laid down — just for a minute.

At 6:15, a line of thunderstorms with small hail and stuff like that went through and woke me up. I went to the Country Table restaurant right next door and had dinner.

Then I went back to the motel. I stopped in the rental office to see if Larry had come home. I asked if I could take a picture of them. They were happy to oblige.

Then, I went to my room and slept like a log.

August 8th
White Pigeon to Kalamazoo, Michigan

I left the Little Country Inn at 8:25 on August 8 and walked down Route 12. Right in front of the motel was a sign pointing the way to Kalamazoo.

Wow! I should be home soon!

At Route 131, I turned to the right and headed north. Just around the corner was the Constantine/Three Rivers sign.

Three miles? That was a cakewalk!

Assuming the distance was right, of course....

Just after coming into Constantine, Route 131 bends sharply to the left. There was a coin-operated laundry on the left side of the road, where I had been walking. The only thing clean in my backpack was one pair of socks. If I were going to continue to walk, I knew I should wash my clothes. But I had been feeling like I had been done for a couple of days.

Once again, I stood unable to make a decision. So I made myself a deal. I would stand on the east side of the road and see if someone would give me a ride the last 35 miles to Kalamazoo. Ten minutes, I decided, is what I would give myself.

After a while, I decided no one was going to pick me up — not that I would blame them. I was sweaty and must not have smelled all that wonderful. Up the road about 50 feet was a big oak tree. I decided to walk up there and sit down. I looked at my watch. I had only been standing there six minutes. "Ten minutes!" I said to myself, "You said ten minutes, not six." I faced south and stuck my thumb out again.

Once again, no one even looked at me. For that matter, hardly anyone went by me going north. I couldn't see any cars coming from the south. The ten minutes had gone by. I shrugged, turned north, and started walking toward the shade under that big oak tree. I hadn't gone very far when Travis Milne stopped and offered me a ride. He was going way up north in Michigan, returning from transporting travel trailers around the country. He drove me right to the entrance to the Lake Forest Apartments, where I live.

While I was standing there in Constantine for that last four minutes, it occurred to me that Moses and the Israelites wandered in the wilderness for 40 years. Jesus, when he was being tempted by Satan, was in the desert for 40 days and 40 nights. Today was the 40th day I had been on the road....

Epilogue

This is where the answers should be, isn't it?

But I don't have any, really, though I did find reinforcement for some of my beliefs.

Apparently, the infotainment industry would like you to believe that most of the people in our country are criminals — murderers, rapists, burglars, muggers, embezzlers, and other scofflaws. I met a lot of people on this journey, and I am happy to report they were all good folks. I made a lot of new friends.

Turn off the TV more often. Listen, really listen, to someone you care about.

If you are a good driver, as you make your way from town to town you will be intent on the traffic around you. You will be attentive to the brake lights of the vehicle in front of you. You'll adjust your radio and/or CD player. You'll probably even talk on your cell phone.

But someday, try this. Drive (or better, walk) five or ten miles outside the suburbs of your home town. Get out of your car and sit by the side of the road. Eventually, the traffic will all go away for a while. What you will see for miles in all directions is the beautiful land we are fortunate to inhabit. With the cars out of sight, I'm sure it looks much as it did before we arrived here. Look at it. Really look at it. Listen to the lowing of cattle in the distance and to the soft sigh of the wind. You may be able to see the breeze moving the grain. You can smell it — almost taste it.

We take this beautiful world for granted. And we do so at our peril, I believe. If we're not careful, we may end up losing it altogether.

Follow your heart.

Notes

After I got home, I sent EMails and letters to people I had met asking them if I could use their names in this book, and asking what they remembered from the time we met. Some of their replies are the notes that follow.

1. As far as my memories of that day, the first one that comes to mind is it was very hot. I remember commenting that we were tired and you said you were even more so. I asked why and you told us about your walking all day. I remember you telling us about having a vision that prompted you to walk all the way back to Michigan. We never got around to asking you for more details about your vision. We should have.
   The other thing I remember is you were a very friendly and literate person. I'm sure your book will be fascinating to read as your e-mails were. I talk to strangers a lot, especially when traveling. Every one has a story, as I am sure you know.
   Keep in touch.
   [Jack Harper]

2. Dear Brother John,
   What a wonderful "serendipity" to hear from you, and that you "finished your course (race)" for the Lord.
   Thanks for being a "walking witness" for Christ, and a happy and holy Christmas to you and your family.
   In Christ,
   Terry Faris, Corbin D.S.

3. The letters   form the Greek word for fish. Transliterated into English, it becomes **ichthys**, which is part of our word **ichthyology**, the scientific study of fish. The letters can be used as an acronym for **Jesus Christ Of God Son Savior**, or **Jesus Christ, Son of God, Savior**.
    — Iota, the first letter in the Greek word **Iesous** Jesus
    — Chi, the first letter in the Greek word **Christos** Christ
    — Theta, the first letter in the Greek word **Theos** Of God
    — Upsilon, the first letter in the Greek word **Yios** (Huois) Son
    — Sigma, the first letter in the Greek word **Soter** Savior

Early Christians were persecuted by Romans and Jews alike. The sign of the fish became sort of an early password. If you thought someone you had just met might be a Christian, you would make a line in the dirt like this.

To complete the password, the other person would draw the other half of the fish like this.

The shape is quick and easy to draw, and if there was any problem, it could be erased just as quickly.

4. Hi John,
We met when you were taking a break by a picnic table outside my office in Renfro Valley, Kentucky. We went to Snyders on hwy 25 for lunch. I was a bit worried about your feet and hiking condition and we had a nice chat sitting at the country café. I was thinking soup beans was the special for the day but I forget if that is what I had. You told me you had received some sort of message to take a walk and meet people. I drive by Synders café every day and take photos of what is the daily special. To jog your memory you could go to this site http://www.dailycommute25.blogspot.com/

I will think some more and tell you more. Sure use my name and the Christian Appalachian project where you stopped and where I teach Adult education.

God Bless you
Keith Gilbertson

5. John,
It was a normal work day in the Admissions office of Berea College. I was working, scheduling visits and fielding any questions that came in. When you walked into the office, I approached you in the way that I would have approached anyone coming in. I was trying to do my job in assisting visitors to our campus. You started by asking a few general questions about Berea and I tried my best to answer them. (Might I say...you knew more than most) As we began talking, you started talking about the dream/challenge God had placed on your heart. At that moment, I felt like I needed to help you in any way possible, and I very quickly began to pray for you and your journey. You began explaining why you were doing what you were doing and you were also talking about the youth that you were gathering information for.

We chatted for what I think was about an hour or so and then we gave you some information about a hotel that you could rest at. Before you left, you mentioned that you were emailing updates and I asked to be added to that list. I wasn't expecting anything different from a normal workday that morning and ended up having a conversation that allowed my faith to shine for many in my office. Also, the whole talking with strangers...I do it often because of the nature of my job; but rarely do we talk in-depth about things that are not directly related to Berea and the admissions requirements.

I hope that you get the opportunity to publish and share your journey with many others.
Laura Sands

6. Good to hear from you. Of course I remember you. The picture was not necessary. Throughout my life I have felt God

sends individuals to me from time to time. I sometimes think of them as Angels but I really know they are just his people He uses in different ways. You are one of those people. I suspect you impacted others as you followed your vision on your walk.

When I was younger (in service and in college) I did some hitchhiking myself. As I obtained my own transportation I picked up hitchhikers on a regular basis. Met some neat people. As times (and I) changed I stopped picking up people because I thought it dangerous. My wife told me that repeatedly. Why I offered you a ride I can not answer. It just seemed right. I just knew you were okay.

You did indeed look worn out. I knew immediately when [you] started talking that you were one of God's angels.

Since meeting with you I have reflected numerous times on our encounter. I realized when you asked what church I attended that I had not been regular in my attendance. I thought about other ways I was not acting like a Christian. Thank you for the "jolt". We all need those periodically.

I hope these random thoughts help and I do think you should finish that book. There are others out there that you can have an impact on!

[Bobby Russell]

7. Hey John,

It is so great to hear from you. I think that your journey was such an inspiration to me. It showed me that with God anything is possible! I think it is so great to see that you are writing a book about your journey. I remember you coming in and sharing your story with us and how happy I was to see someone actually listening to what God has told them and going for it. With such a long journey to go on your hands and the pain to your feet I felt so helpless. I wondered while you were staying with us if there was anything that could be done to help you, but unfortunately there was not a whole lot that I could possibly do since I'm not a doctor or anything. I did pray for your safe journey back home everyday though. And I was so glad to receive your e-mail that you had made it home!!! I felt great inspiration by your journey to seek God a little more than I had and I thank God that you had stopped into my family's hotel because your story was just what I needed for me to feel that God really is there.

I think it is so wonderful that you are writing a book about your journey. Thank you for sending me an e-mail and letting me know how things are going with you!!

God Bless,
Ashley

8. Hello John!

Of course I remember you! It was in July of this year on the first day of my orientation to a new home-care job. It was a little cool that day and I believe it rained. I was taking advantage of the hotel's free breakfast bar when I ran into an acquaintance. The mother of a former Tae Kwon Do student that my oldest son and I trained with happened to work at that particular hotel. I told her why I was there and upon learning that I was a nurse she told me about your feet. To answer your question about [whether I often talk] to strangers the answer is "YES!" To be honest with you it's hard for me to ever meet a stranger if you know what I mean. I have always been very talkative and outgoing so I make friends very easily. I never mind helping anyone in need. We all can use a little professional free advise from time to time. I hope that your feet healed enough for you to continue your journey through life both figurative and literally. Since I met you unfortunately the nice couple that owned the home-care job that I began to work for decided to sell their business in October. I've been unhappily unemployed since then. I have been looking for the right job. I am praying that God will guide me in the right direction and allow me to use my talents properly. Unfortunately, I am not perfect and I have made mistakes in my life that are making my employment difficult. I have also had some unexpected health problems to deal with-but I'm not dying and as one patient once told me

'Every day above the ground is a good day!' I was an art major before I became a nurse so if you need art-work for your book I'll be happy to help. If I could do freelance art as a full-time profession I would. Good Bye and God Bless!

    Jenny Dininger :)

9.   I remember that day pretty fluently, a hot summer day just after lunch time when you were walking in. I was at teller station four when you approached me. I believe you were getting money out to eat when we began to chat. I wouldn't necessarily call anyone a stranger who comes into the bank, I meet new people everyday and I enjoy that. Some are very polite like yourself, and others you could rather have not met them. Everyone with problems with their accounts blame it on us the tellers when we never even mess their accounts up. But anyways I like meeting new people. You told me all about the journey you had before you and I was amazed that you were actually walking that. I don't even think I could drive that far. It's good to know that you are so dedicated for your church to walk all the way from Tennessee to Michigan. Thank you again for writing me and letting me know about your successful trip.

    [Andrew Bowley]

10. John, I met you this summer a little north of Cincinnati at the Subway I work at inside of the Wal-Mart. Sorry, I do not remember the exact sandwich I made you, ha. You were at the Wal-Mart getting medicines for your feet which had been hurting you pretty bad at that point. We talked about your trip thus far and we also talked about your vision that made you decide to do it. I often make small talk with my customers, usually just to make the day go faster, but there was something interesting about you. I had a feeling that you were actually 'doing' something other than getting a sandwich on a hot summer day. The funny thing is that the night before I met you, I had watched part of and had a dream about the movie Forest Gump. I noticed the cross you were wearing and your giant beard and thought, "wouldn't it be crazy if this guy was just 'running'?" It's kind of funny how things like that happen. I told a bunch of my friends about you as well as my parents. Ha, I'm not sure if they believe me about my dream the night before. Anyway, I hope the rest of your trip went well and your feet are still working for you. It was good to have met you. Take care.

    Clint E.

11. You can find Ortberg's editorial at: http://www.christianitytoday.com/leaders/newsletter/2002/cln20704.html

12. Hi John ---
    How could I forget you???
    I was having breakfast at the Holiday Inn Express near Mason, Ohio.
    The thing that struck me was how familiar you seemed to be with the hostess. I thought at first you must be a frequent visitor, or maybe a relative of hers. I was surprised to find out that you were just traveling through.
    I wasn't intentionally eavesdropping; however, I soon caught the topic of conversation. Since I am a retired salesman and spent many a lonely night on the road, I joined in the conversation to learn more about your travels. I remember my last words to you: "You know, you really should consider writing a book". I'm sure you heard that more than once!
    My wife and I were there attending a baseball tournament involving our oldest son (one of the coaches) and our grandson (one of the players). We enjoy following the team to various cities and towns. The experiences are invaluable for all of the families involved.
    Finally, you had a dramatic effect on the start of my day. Your personal witness continues to give credence to everything and anything is possible with the help of the Lord.
    I printed out your emails and have shared them with the Habitat for Humanity Hamilton County (Indiana) "Tiger" team.

The "Tiger" team is a group of 12 retired men who work on Habitat houses twice a week. As you know, Habitat is a Christian based organization. Your story has found a home with us.

Larry G.

13. Hi John

Jami Murray here, from Bluffton Indiana. My husband Dan and I and our 2 daughters Taylor and Lexi met you at Walmart in Decatur Indiana at the check out line. I first saw you in the store, because your camelback you were wearing caught my eye. My husband and I were getting ready to head on a 500 mile bicycle trip to West Virginia with our church and before that I had no idea what a camelback was. So I questioned in my mind, what you were doing, where you were going and whence you came.

You answered those questions when we met in the check out lane. You were buying new socks for your next trek. Thanks for sharing your story, it was a real inspiration to us, knowing you were walking and we, some years younger, were riding for the same reasons, Christ our Lord and to help others!

Spreading the Word and Staying in Shape

The Murray's

14. If you're curious about Coffindaffer Crosses, check out these links:

http://www.christiancrosses.org/History.htm

http://www.wvgazette.com/static/century/gz1008.html

http://www.christiancrosses.org/CperState.htm

15. hey john

i'm glad to hear you made it home and yes you are in my prayers I am sorry it has taken me this long to reply I am having a lot of family trouble right now and I am trying to get my life back on track all I can do is pray my baby turned a year old on October the 17th he has gotten really big I will try and send you a picture of the children ok god bless

[Charlene Johnson].

Printed in the United States
113599LV00003B